THE BARBECUE COOKBOOK

Joanna White

BRISTOL PUBLISHING ENTERPRISES
San Leandro, California

A nitty gritty® Cookbook

Printed in the United States of America.

ISBN: 1-55867-260-5

Cover design: Frank J. Paredes
Cover photography: John A. Benson
Food stylist: Susan Devaty
Illustrations: James Balkovek

CONTENTS

ABOUT BARBECUING AND GRILLING

The sizzling aromas and flavors of barbecued meats have been enjoyed for over 100,000 years. Grilling or barbecuing outdoors is fun and relaxing, and lends itself to easy entertaining. It requires very little fat, and the high heat seals in natural moisture, transforming ordinary meat into a delicacy suffused with flavor. Grilling reduces fat intake, since much of the fat drips away from the food. In this book are recipes for all types of meat, poultry, fish, vegetables and fruit as well as marinades, compound butters, spice rubs and sauces. Included is information about barbecuing techniques, types of grills available, safety and cleaning methods. Barbecuing should be fun, not a chore. Enjoy delicious, laid-back dining and relax with your family and friends.

BARBECUING VERSUS GRILLING

Grilling is basically cooking over the coals without a cover. The coals on the open grill are hotter and more prone to flare-ups. This makes the food cook quickly and the outside become slightly charred. Charring seals in juices, but leaves the inside succulent and tender. This technique is best for foods which are up to $1\frac{1}{2}$ inches thick. The best foods for grilling are steaks, chops, fish fillets, shellfish, skewered food, vegetable slices and poultry without the skin. Poultry with the skin on tends to produce too much fat. This creates flare-ups that heavily chars the outside of the food and does not cook the inside sufficiently.

Barbecuing means cooking on a closed grill: the heat circulates all around the food, cooking it evenly and creating a more "smoky" flavor. Ideal foods for this method are roasts, chicken, duck, thick fish steaks and whole vegetables. Generally, if the food tends to dry out on the grill, cook it covered. Use this method if you are having too many flare-ups from either fatty foods or foods that are basted with an oily marinade.

TYPES OF BARBECUES AND GRILLS

Brazier: Otherwise known as an open grill, this does not have a cover. It is usually round, with a single cooking rack supported by a central spindle, and is designed for direct heat cooking. Be sure to buy one that has sturdy legs so the grill will not topple over. Drippings can cause flare-ups, so try to allow coals to burn to medium-hot before grilling and keep a spray bottle of water handy.

Electric Countertop Grill: This stick-resistant grill is electrically heated to preset temperatures. This is used for indoor grilling.

Electric Smoker: An electrically heated box smokes and cooks food on wire shelves by indirect heat. Fragrant wood chips reproduce the effects of a traditional pit barbecue.

A cold smoker is used to smoke food without exposing it to direct heat. Generally the meat is soaked in brine or cure to help draw out the moisture because the temperature in the cold smoker is usually between 90° and 130° and the food is not considered fully cooked. Additional cooking is necessary for foods such as ham or bacon.

Smoke cooking uses both heat and smoke to cook the food. The temperature is generally between 170° and 250°, which is needed to kill bacteria and prevent mold growth. Curing is not necessary when using this method.

Gas Grill: Enameled grids or lava rocks are heated by propane gas burners. The drippings are vaporized to produce smoke and the grease is channeled off to prevent flare-ups. The advantages of a gas grill are instant cooking and longer barbecuing time without having to add more charcoal, but some say the flavor is somewhat compromised. Using presoaked wood chips directly on the lava stones will make up for some of the flavor lost in not grilling on charcoal. Gas grills generally cook at temperatures between 700° and 900°, slightly hotter than briquettes. A pan of water placed on the grill will help to create steam when the lid is down, which really keeps the meat moist.

Hibachi: This small Japanese-style grill is designed for direct heat cooking methods and is limited to cooking for 2 to 3 people. It is useful for those with limited space or for traveling.

Kamado: This egg-shaped Japanese smoker is made of very heavy earthenware with a hinged lid. It bakes and smokes simultaneously and can be used as an open grill if desired. The kamado cooks evenly and keeps the food inside deliciously moist.

Kettle Grill: A dome-shaped grill is designed for closed-hood grilling. It can act as a smoker, oven and grill. You can choose between gas, charcoal and electric versions. Some come with shelves and/or side burners for cooking side dishes. The rounded base and hood reflect heat off all inside surfaces, which cooks food quickly and evenly. The domed cover is vented for temperature control and can be used for indirect cooking as well as direct-heat grilling.

Stovetop Grill: A stick-resistant indoor cooktop grill is domed and vented to drain off fat into a water-filled drip pan.

Water Smoker: A covered grill allows you to cook over indirect heat. It uses a long, slow cooking method of sprinkling the fire with dampened wood chunks to create steamy clouds of wood smoke which penetrate the food. Some come with a pan positioned between the fuel grate and the cooking rack for holding water. It is suitable for outdoor smoking, steaming, grilling and roasting and uses charcoal, gas or electricity. The internal temperature usually stays around 160° to 200°. You'll need to add more coals and/or wood chips about every 45 minutes to keep the smoker going.

GENERAL INFORMATION

Utensils: Essentials for grilling are long-handled tongs, spatulas and forks, basting brushes and heavy hand mitts. Other hand accessories include special grilling baskets that are used for delicate fish, small fruits and vegetables (to prevent food from falling through the grill), skewers, spray water bottle, wire brush and spark lighter. I personally always use an instant thermometer to guarantee the proper temperature of large grilled meats such as roasts and birds. To use this thermometer effectively, the meat should be at least 2 inches thick.

Charcoal grill technique: The ideal method is to line the firebox with a double layer of heavy aluminum foil and add 1 inch of pea gravel (this will create good air circulation). To determine the amount of coals needed, spread charcoal briquettes on top of the gravel in a single layer extending 1 inch outside the edge of the food. Then push the coals into a pile and light. Self-lighting coals will take about 8 minutes before they are ready for grilling. Standard coals require about 25 to 30 minutes before they are ready. Coals are ready when they appear gray (during the day) or glowing red all over (in evening light). Be aware that some briquettes may have a higher filler or chemical additive content that may create an unpleasant taste or greasy residue. Make sure these coals have a gray ash coating before grilling. I like to lightly brush the hot grill rack with oil before cooking to discourage food from sticking.

Hardwood charcoal: This charcoal is made directly from whole pieces of wood with no additives or fillers, just pure charcoal. The most common woods used are mesquite, maple, cherry, oak and hickory. These tend to burn hotter and cleaner than briquettes and leave no unpleasant taste. They generally burn at temperatures 200° to 300° hotter than briquettes and are reusable. Larger chunks may need to be broken down into smaller, more uniform pieces before igniting.

Wood chips: These woods include mesquite, alder, hickory, oak, apple, cherry and peach. Add chips to the heated briquettes to give food a special wood-smoked flavor. Often the wood should be soaked before using: be sure to read instructions on the bag.

Dried grapevines can be used without soaking; they give off a subtle, sweet smoke. Wood from fruit trees creates a sweet smoke that works well with poultry. Pork goes well with hickory and pecan woods, and white alder is ideal for seafood.

Fire starters: The easiest briquettes are the self-lighting variety: simply light with a match to start. To fire up other types of briquettes, you may use electric starters, liquid starters, wax starters or jelly starters. Be sure to allow the fire starters to soak into the briquettes for at least 1 minute before igniting. *Never* use gasoline or kerosene to start the coals and never add starter after the fire has started. Chimney fire starters are loaded with charcoal on top and crumpled newspaper in the bottom. Ignite the paper and set: the coals are ready in about 20 minutes.

Direct cooking: Spread the coals evenly in a single layer. Place food directly on the grill over the coals. If flare-ups occur, spread the coals about 1/2 inch apart, remove some of the coals and raise the grill rack or cover the grill.

Indirect cooking: Place a disposable foil drip pan in the center of the coals and mound the coals around the outside edge. This prevents the juices from dripping onto the coals and causing flare-ups.

Temperature: To determine temperature for direct heat, hold your hand over the grill at the level the food will be cooked. For hot, you should be able to hold your hand over the coals for 2 seconds, 3 seconds for medium-hot, 4 seconds for medium, 5 seconds for medium-low and 6 seconds for low. For indirect cooking, you'll need to slightly increase the temperature, for example hot coals for medium-high heat and so forth.

General cooking instructions: Most of the dishes in this book have been prepared on a gas grill with a nonmovable grill rack fixed at about 6 inches above the fuel grate. All the food was brought to room temperature before grilling. The type of charcoal can make a difference in the temperature—mesquite charcoal has a tendency to burn slightly hotter than briquettes—so cooking time may vary slightly depending on your grill and the type of fuel you use.

To turn off the grill: Immediately after the food is removed, cover the grill and close down all the vents. This will remove the oxygen and extinguish the coals. This technique is ideal for hardwood charcoal since it is reusable. For open grills simply douse the coals lightly with water. If using hardwood charcoal, allow the coals to dry thoroughly and reuse with fresh coals for your next barbecue. Turn off the switches on your gas grill, and make sure the main propane bottle is turned off completely.

Cleaning the grill: Ideally, clean your grill right after cooking. Allow the grill to soak in hot, sudsy water while eating and simply wipe clean. Grill brushes are available for removing burnt-on food.

SAFETY ADVICE

1. Move the grill away from your house. Avoid grilling under trees or near dry leaves.
2. If you are using a portable grill, do not cook on the tailgate of your vehicle.
3. Watch the grill at all times. Do not leave unattended, especially with children around.
4. Before grilling have all your tools ready and next to the grill, especially heavy

mitts and a water spray bottle.

5. Keep the grill clean: the charred build-up encourages food to stick and takes away from the flavor. Clean the rack well with a wire brush, wipe off with a towel and lightly brush with oil before grilling. A towel soaked with oil is handy for wiping.
6. It is always best to empty the ash-catcher before grilling to assist oxygen flow around the coals.
7. Keep children and pets away from hot grills and equipment.
8. It's not a bad idea to keep a fire extinguisher nearby in case of emergency.
9. Never use gasoline or kerosene to start a fire and never use starter after the fire is going.
10. Do not grill indoors unless the unit is specifically designed for it.
11. Avoid grilling in windy areas.
12. Be careful when using grills that allow embers to fall through vents onto a wooden deck or the grass. Either wet the area well before grilling or position a large metal pan directly under the grill.
13. Never attempt to move a hot grill.
14. Avoid dumping coals and/or ashes in a place where they might start a fire or along a pathway where people or animals walk.

APPETIZERS

11   Grilled Garlic Bulbs
12   Chicken Buffalo Wings
13   Cheese Quesadillas
14   Asian Mini-Ribs
15   Ginger Plum Drumettes
16   Grilled Clams and Mussels
17   Grilled Cheese in Grape Leaves
18   Lime Chicken Soup
20   Grilled Tomato and Cheese Pizza
22   Portobello Mushroom Bruschetta
24   Grilled Oysters with Spicy Butter

GRILLED GARLIC BULBS

Servings: 8-12
Grill: Medium

Garlic bulbs are usually covered with aluminum or cooked in a covered dish. This recipe allows you to cook directly on the grill and requires much less cooking time. For variations try mixing any combination of herbs and/or spices in the olive oil to enhance the taste even more.

3 full bulbs garlic
olive oil for brushing
1 loaf dense Italian bread, cut in 3/4-inch thick slices
crushed rosemary and/or black pepper for seasoning, optional

Remove most of the skin from garlic bulb (do not separate cloves). Liberally brush bulbs with olive oil. Fire up the grill and when coals are at medium, place oiled bulbs on grill and cook, turning several times until cloves are soft to the touch and outsides are somewhat charred, about 15 to 20 minutes. Brush one side of bread slice with plain olive oil or olive oil mixed with seasoning of choice. Grill on medium heat until toasted on both sides. Cut the top off garlic bulb and allow guests to squeeze out paste from each clove onto grilled bread.

CHICKEN BUFFALO WINGS

Servings: 6
Grill: Medium-hot

These marinated wings are often served with celery sticks and blue cheese dressing. The amount of Tabasco Sauce will determine how spicy your wings will be.

1 cup cider vinegar
3 tbs. olive oil
2 tbs. Worcestershire sauce
2 tbs. chili powder
$1/2$ tsp. minced fresh garlic

1 tsp. red pepper flakes
1 tsp. salt
$3/4$ tsp. black pepper, or more to taste
1 tsp.–1 tbs. Tabasco Sauce, or to taste
4 lb. chicken wings

In a large locking plastic bag, place vinegar, olive oil, Worcestershire sauce, chili powder, garlic, red pepper, salt, black pepper and Tabasco Sauce and shake to combine. Cut wing tips off chicken wings and discard. Cut remaining pieces at the joint and place in bag. Massage bag to coat pieces completely. Refrigerate for up to 24 hours. Fire up the grill and heat coals to medium-hot. Thoroughly drain marinade from wings and grill wings, turning frequently, for about 25 minutes. Each time you turn wings, baste with the remaining marinade.

CHEESE QUESADILLAS

Servings: 6
Grill: Medium

Quesadillas are extremely popular. Endless variations can be made by adding different types of cooked meats, crumbled cooked bacon, sautéed onions, a variety of fresh herbs, or different types of cheese.

6 eight-inch flour tortillas
olive oil for brushing
1 cup shredded Monterey Jack cheese
1 cup shredded medium-sharp cheddar
  cheese

1/4 cup chopped green onion
1/2 cup mild or hot salsa
3 tbs. chopped fresh cilantro

Brush 3 of the tortillas with olive oil on one side. Place oil-side down on a baking sheet. Mix together Monterey Jack and cheddar cheeses. Evenly distribute cheese, green onion, salsa and cilantro over tortillas and cover with remaining tortillas. Brush oil over top tortillas. Cook quesadillas by indirect grilling. Place an aluminum pan under the center of the grill and arrange coals around outside edges. Fire up grill and when coals are at medium, place quesadillas on grill over pan (not over coals). Close the lid and cook for about 2 minutes, turn once and grill for an additional 2 minutes or until cheese is melted. Remove from grill and cut each quesadilla into 6 wedges. Serve with guacamole and sour cream.

ASIAN MINI-RIBS

Servings: 8
Grill: Medium

Ask your butcher to cut whole slabs of ribs crosswise at 1½-inch intervals. After the ribs are barbecued, cut the meat between ribs to make little "riblets" to serve as appetizers. Most major grocery stores now have an Asian section with the ingredients necessary for this recipe. Otherwise you'll have to make a trip to Chinatown.

¼ cup dark soy sauce
¼ cup dry sherry
2 tbs. hoisin sauce
2 tbs. sugar
1 tbs. ground bean sauce

1 tsp. minced fresh garlic
1 tsp. grated fresh ginger
⅓ tsp. five-spice powder
3 lb. pork spareribs, cut into strips
   horizontally

In a bowl, combine soy sauce, sherry, hoisin sauce, sugar, bean sauce, garlic, ginger and five-spice powder. Pour marinade over rib strips and marinate at room temperature for 30 minutes before grilling. Fire up the grill and when coals are at medium, place ribs on grill, cover, vent to keep temperature reduced and cook for about 45 minutes to 1 hour. These mini-ribs won't take as long as most ribs. Ribs are ready when meat is tender and no pink color remains. Cut meat between bone into individual mini-ribs. Hint: When only using part of a can for recipes that you don't make often, place unused portion in a glass jar, cover with a thin layer of oil, screw on the lid and refrigerate until you need it again.

GINGER PLUM DRUMETTES

These are hot, sweet chicken wings "with a little handle." Only the upper arm of the wing is used and the meat is scraped part way down the bone to make the handle. Once the little drumettes are made, the rest is easy.

1/3 cup peanut or extra virgin olive oil
1/3 cup dry sherry
1/3 cup light soy sauce
2 tbs. bottled plum sauce
1 tbs. grated fresh ginger
1 tbs. minced cilantro

2–3 tsp. hot chili paste
1 1/2 tsp. minced fresh garlic
1 pinch salt
3 lb. chicken drumettes, upper section
   only and scraped to expose bone

In a small bowl, combine oil, sherry, soy sauce, plum sauce, ginger, cilantro, chili paste, garlic and salt. Transfer this liquid to a locking plastic bag and add chicken drumettes, mixing well to distribute marinade. Seal and refrigerate for at least 2 hours, turning the bag occasionally. Remove chicken from the refrigerator about 1/2 hour before grilling. Fire up the grill and when coals are at medium, place drained drumettes on grill, cover and cook for 5 minutes. Turn and baste every 5 minutes until drumettes are well browned, about 15 minutes total cooking time. Watch for flare-ups; adjust vents to help control the amount of fire. Test doneness by cutting through one drumette to make sure the meat has an opaque color throughout.

GRILLED CLAMS AND MUSSELS

This makes a great, easy, almost foolproof appetizer because you know exactly when the clams and mussels are ready. If you plan to serve this as a main course, you should calculate about 1½ lb. per person.

1½ lb. littleneck or manila clams
1 lb. medium mussels
water to cover
¼ cup cornmeal or flour
2 large tomatoes, finely chopped
3 tbs. finely chopped onion
2 tbs. finely chopped fresh cilantro

2 tbs. extra virgin olive oil
1 tsp. grated lemon zest
¾ tsp. dried oregano
½ tsp. minced fresh garlic
½ tsp. salt
¼ tsp. black pepper

Scrub clams and mussels, and remove any beards from mussels. Place cleaned clams and mussels in a bowl of water with cornmeal or flour added. Refrigerate for 1 to 2 hours, shaking bowl occasionally to help expel gritty sand. Mix remaining ingredients together in a separate bowl. Taste and adjust seasonings. Fire up the grill and when coals are hot, place well-drained clams and mussels on grill. Note: If clams or mussels are too small, use a grill basket to cook on so clams won't fall through grill. Cook for about 4 to 5 minutes or until shells are open. Discard any unopened shells! Spoon fresh sauce over cooked clams and mussels and serve immediately.

GRILLED CHEESE IN GRAPE LEAVES

Any good cheese you would serve on bread—except perhaps cheddar—will work in this recipe. Serve with crusty French bread, focaccia, or one of the new exotic breads now available, like garlic/rosemary bread, herb bread or olive bread.

3/4 cup extra virgin olive oil
1 tbs. chopped fresh rosemary or basil, or 1 tsp. dried
1 tsp. minced fresh garlic
black pepper to taste

large bottled grape leaves for wrapping
olive oil for rubbing
8 oz. Parmesan or Romano cheese or goat cheese rounds

In a small bowl, combine olive oil, rosemary, garlic and pepper. Drain grape leaves and pat dry. If using hard cheese like Parmesan, rub leaves with olive oil and stack 3 on top of each other. Place a thick slice (about 1/2-inch) cheese on the leaves, brush with marinade and place open-faced on the grill so cheese will take on a smoky flavor. If using a soft cheese, pour marinade over cheese, cover and refrigerate overnight. Rub leaves with olive oil, overlap leaves in a circle, remove cheese from marinade and place in the center of leaves. Completely cover cheese with leaves. Fire up the grill and when coals are at medium, place cheese packets on grill and cover. For open-face cheese, cook for about 3 minutes and remove. For enclosed cheese packets, place on cooler section of grill, cover and cook for about 3 minutes per side.

LIME CHICKEN SOUP

Servings: 6
Grill: Medium-hot

This tropical soup is loaded with flavor. Serve with crusty bread, crisp crackers or tortilla chips. This would go well with a colorful vegetable salad and a creamy flan for dessert.

2 tbs. olive oil
1 1/4 cups diced red or Walla Walla sweet onions
1 tbs. minced fresh garlic
1 tsp.–1 tbs. minced, deseeded jalapeño peppers, to taste
1/4 tsp. ground cinnamon, or to taste
6 cups chicken stock
3/4 cup diced tomatoes
1/4 cup lime juice
3 boneless, skinless chicken breast halves
1 1/2 tbs. olive oil
2 tbs. ground cumin
salt and black pepper to taste

In a saucepan, heat oil over medium heat and add onions. Sauté until onions are wilted and transparent, about 5 minutes. Add garlic, jalapeños and cinnamon and cook for 1 minute longer, making sure not to brown garlic. Reduce heat to low, add chicken stock, tomatoes, and lime juice and simmer for about 10 minutes. Pound chicken breasts between two sheets of waxed paper until meat is all the same thickness. Brush breasts with olive oil and rub in cumin, salt and pepper.

Fire up the grill and when coals are medium-hot, oil grill rack and cook chicken for about 6 to 7 minutes per side. Meat should be opaque in the center with no pink color. Cut chicken into bite-sized pieces. Add chicken pieces to soup and simmer for about 8 minutes. Taste and adjust seasonings. Add more jalapeños or a dash of Tabasco Sauce if you like it hot; add more lime juice if you like it sour. Adjust salt and pepper to your personal taste.

GRILLED TOMATO AND CHEESE PIZZA

Pizza dough can be grilled on the barbecue! Use any combination of vegetables, cheeses and herbs that appeals to you. Goat cheese is extremely popular and goes well with grilled chicken, marinated artichoke hearts and a sprinkling of thyme.

1 tbs. (1 envelope) dry yeast
1 1/2 cups warm water
1 tbs. extra virgin olive oil
1 1/2 tsp. sugar or honey
4 cups flour
2/3 cup whole-wheat flour
1 1/2 tsp. salt
1/4 cup extra virgin olive oil, divided
6-8 red or yellow plum tomatoes, sliced or chopped
6 oz. whole milk mozzarella, fontina or Monterey Jack cheese, grated
1/3 cup grated Romano cheese
1 tsp. minced fresh garlic, or more to taste
1 cup coarsely chopped fresh basil leaves or cilantro

In a bowl, stir together yeast, warm water, olive oil and sugar and let stand until mixture begins to bubble slightly, about 5 minutes. Using a wooden spoon, beat flour, whole-wheat flour and salt into yeast mix. Remove dough from bowl and place on a floured board. Knead dough until smooth but still somewhat sticky. Place mixture into an oiled bowl, cover and let rise in a warm place until doubled in bulk, about 2 hours. Cut dough into 4 pieces, flour a cookie sheet and roll dough into circles about 1/8-inch thick (the baking sheet should hold 2 pieces).

Fire up the grill and when coals are hot, brush grill rack with oil and slide one round of dough onto the grill. Cook for 1 minute or until underside of pizza is browned. Turn dough over using tongs and grill for about 1/2 minute or until underside of dough begins to stiffen. Repeat on the 3 remaining rounds. Brush pizzas with olive oil, sprinkle 1/2 of the cheese on top, and then tomatoes, garlic and basil. Top with remaining cheese. Reduce heat to medium and grill covered, a few at a time, for 2 minutes or until cheese melts. Cut into slices and serve immediately.

Watch very carefully to make sure bottom of pizza doesn't burn during this last step. If it looks like it will burn, place a pan or pizza stone under dough to protect it while cheese melts.

PORTOBELLO MUSHROOM BRUSCHETTA

Servings: 4
Grill: Hot

Portobello mushrooms are meaty, flavorful and huge! Bruschetta is bread that is toasted or grilled and topped with a flavorful spread usually made of vegetables. If fresh basil is not available, bottled pesto, which is now readily available in stores, can be substituted for the first 6 ingredients.

$1/2$ cup fresh basil leaves, packed
3 tbs. grated Parmesan cheese
1 tbs. pine nuts
$1/2$ tsp. minced fresh garlic
salt and pepper to taste, divided
2 tbs. extra virgin olive oil
4 portobello mushrooms
2 tbs. olive oil for brushing
$1/4$ tsp. lemon juice
12 small slices dense country bread
shredded Romano or Parmesan cheese for garnish

With a food processor or blender, combine basil leaves, Parmesan cheese, pine nuts, garlic, salt and pepper. Process this mixture by pulsing into a coarse puree. With the machine running, slowly pour olive oil into mixture and blend until thickened. Taste and adjust seasonings. Remove stems from mushrooms and wipe with a towel to remove any specks. In a small bowl, mix together olive oil and lemon juice. Brush this mixture on mushrooms and sprinkle liberally with salt and pepper.

Fire up the grill and when coals are hot, brush grill rack with oil and cook mushrooms for about 3 to 5 minutes per side or until tender. Brush rack again with oil and grill bread slices for about 1 minute on each side until toasted. Slice mushrooms into thin strips.

Spread toasted bread with pesto, lay slices of mushroom over pesto and sprinkle with a little shredded Romano or Parmesan cheese. Serve hot.

GRILLED OYSTERS WITH SPICY BUTTER

Servings: 6
Grill: Hot

Oysters are extremely easy to grill and can have endless combinations of basting butters or sauces to enhance their flavor. As an appetizer calculate 2 to 3 per person depending on size. As an entrée, calculate 6 medium or large oysters per person.

$^1/_2$ cup butter
$1^1/_2$ tbs. dry white wine, lime juice or tequila
1 tsp. minced fresh garlic
$^1/_3$ tsp. cayenne pepper
$^1/_4$–$^1/_2$ tsp. Tabasco Sauce, to taste
salt to taste
2–3 dozen large oysters

In a saucepan, heat butter on low heat and whisk in wine, garlic, cayenne pepper, Tabasco Sauce and salt. Taste and adjust seasonings and keep warm until oysters are ready. Scrub oysters with a wire brush. Fire up the grill and when coals are hot, place oysters on grill and cook until they open. Note: Be careful—they spit hot liquid! Have an oyster knife and towels ready for shucking oysters. Drizzle a little butter sauce on oysters before serving or serve alongside.

MARINADES AND RUBS

PORK APPLE MARINADE

Apple is the perfect compliment to pork—I almost always serve applesauce as an accompaniment to pork dishes. This marinade can also be used with chicken and duck.

2/3 cup apple juice
1/4 cup honey
1/4 cup soy sauce
2 1/2 tbs. lemon juice
1 tsp. minced fresh garlic
1/2 tsp. Dijon mustard
1/4 tsp. ground ginger
2 1/2 lb. pork, chicken or duck

In a bowl, mix apple juice, honey, soy sauce, lemon, garlic, mustard and ginger and pour into a locking plastic bag. Add pork and massage bag thoroughly to coat the meat. Refrigerate at least 4 hours before grilling meat.

LAMB MINT MARINADE

Mint is my favorite flavor compliment to lamb. Try serving a little mint jelly with your grilled lamb—it's delicious.

3 tbs. butter, melted
1 cup dry white wine
1/3 cup honey
2 tbs. apple cider vinegar
1 tbs. chopped fresh mint, or 1 tsp. dried
1 tsp. minced fresh garlic
1/2 tsp. salt
2 1/2–3 lb. lamb

In a small bowl, combine butter, white wine, honey, vinegar, mint, garlic and salt. Pour mixture into a locking plastic bag and add lamb, mixing well. Refrigerate for at least 4 hours before grilling lamb.

BEEF TERIYAKI MARINADE

Makes 1³/₄ cups

This marinade can also be used for chicken or pork. If time permits, this recipe tastes better if marinated overnight. For a garnish, sprinkle your cooked meat with sesame seeds. If you wish a more delicate teriyaki flavor use the lighter variety of soy sauce.

²/₃ cup soy sauce
¹/₂ cup vegetable oil
¹/₃ cup finely minced green onion
¹/₃ cup honey
¹/₄ cup dry sherry
2¹/₂ tsp. grated fresh ginger, or ³/₄ tsp. ground
1 tsp. minced fresh garlic
3 lb. beef, chicken or pork

In a small bowl, mix soy sauce, oil, onion, honey, sherry, ginger and garlic and transfer to a locking plastic bag. Place meat in locking plastic bag, massage well to coat meat and refrigerate for at least 4 hours.

POULTRY WINE MARINADE

Here is a great marinade for chicken or turkey. If using poultry with the skin, it helps to make a few deep slits with a knife through the skin into the meat to help the marinade infuse the meat.

½ cup dry white wine
¼ cup cider vinegar
1 medium onion, chopped
2 tbs. olive oil
1½ tbs. lemon juice
1 tsp. honey
1 tsp. minced fresh garlic
1 tsp. grated lemon juice
¾ tsp. dried thyme leaves
½ tsp. black pepper
1 pinch cayenne pepper
3 lb. poultry

Place all of the ingredients in a food processor workbowl or blender container and puree until smooth. Pour into a locking plastic bag, add poultry and massage ingredients to distribute marinade. Refrigerate at least 4 hours or overnight.

WILD GAME ORANGE MARINADE

Orange sauce and marinades go well with game because the more intense flavor covers the stronger flavor of game meats. This marinade would complement duck, all types of game birds, rabbit and pork.

¼ cup butter
1 cup orange juice
⅓ cup honey
2½ tbs. balsamic vinegar
2 tbs. soy sauce
1½ tbs. minced fresh rosemary leaves, or 1½ tsp. dried
1 tbs. Dijon mustard
2 tsp. minced fresh garlic
2 tsp. minced fresh ginger, or ¾ tsp. ground
salt and pepper to taste
4 lb. duck, game birds, rabbit or pork

Melt butter in a saucepan and add orange juice, honey, balsamic vinegar, soy sauce, rosemary, mustard, garlic, ginger, salt and pepper. Heat on medium-low for 5 minutes. Taste and adjust seasonings. Cool to room temperature, transfer to a locking plastic bag, add game meat and mix well. Refrigerate for at least 4 hours before grilling.

INDIAN YOGURT MARINADE

Makes 1³/₄ cups

This marinade has a thick consistency, so you'll need to use more to cover the meat. It works well with chicken, lamb, beef and game birds. Because the skin of fowl will prevent the flavor infusing the meat, you must make several deep slits through the skin and into the meat to insure proper penetration of flavor.

1½ cups plain yogurt
¼ cup extra virgin olive oil
3 tbs. chopped mint leaves
1½ tbs. fresh lemon juice
2¼ tsp. ground fenugreek
2 tsp. sugar
1¼ tsp. ground cardamom
1 tsp. minced fresh garlic
¼–½ tsp. black pepper to taste
2½–3 lb. chicken, lamb or beef

In a bowl, combine yogurt, olive oil, mint, lemon, fenugreek, sugar, cardamom, garlic and pepper. Taste and adjust seasonings. Spread meat with marinade, cover and refrigerate for a minimum of 4 hours or overnight for best flavor.

APRICOT AND WINE MARINADE

This is an excellent marinade for more delicately flavored meats such as veal, poultry and pork. It has a sweet and fruity flavor.

1 1/2 cups sweet red Marsala wine
1/4 cup extra virgin olive oil
1/4 cup orange marmalade
1 tsp. chopped fresh thyme, or 1/3 tsp. dried
1/4 tsp. black pepper, or more to taste
3–4 lb. veal, poultry or pork

With a food processor or blender, puree wine, olive oil, marmalade, thyme and pepper until smooth. Taste and adjust seasonings. Place meat in a glass or other nonreactive baking dish, pour marinade on top, cover and refrigerate for at least 3 to 4 hours.

TERIYAKI MARINADE

Makes 1 1/2 cups

This is a standard version of teriyaki marinade that goes well with all types of meats and seafood. The unusual ingredient is mirin, which is now available in most major grocery stores. It is a Japanese sweet rice wine. Be sure to buy the unseasoned variety. Teriyaki can be used as a marinade, a stir-fry sauce and a dipping sauce. If mirin is not available, replace with sweet sherry.

2/3 cup soy sauce
1/2 cup unseasoned mirin rice wine
3 tbs. brown sugar
2 tbs. minced fresh ginger
1 tsp. minced fresh garlic
1 1/2 tsp. toasted sesame oil
2–3 lb. all types meat or seafood

Place soy sauce, mirin, sugar, ginger, garlic and sesame oil in a food processor workbowl or blender container and blend until well mixed. Pour over meat of choice, cover and refrigerate for at least 4 hours or overnight. If marinating seafood, only marinate for 1/2 hour at room temperature or 2 hours maximum in the refrigerator.

MEAT OR FISH SPICE RUB

Makes ½ cup

This is a garlic-flavored spicy rub that can be mild or hot, depending on the amount of cayenne pepper. As always, try to use fresh herbs whenever possible. I've given the amount of dried herbs that can be substituted.

3 tbs. minced fresh parsley, or 1 tbs. dried
2 tbs. minced fresh oregano, or 2 tsp. dried
1½ tsp. minced fresh rosemary, or ½ tsp. dried
1¼ tsp. minced fresh thyme leaves, or scant ½ tsp. dried
1 tbs. minced fresh garlic, or to taste
1 tbs. dried beef bouillon, or 3 crumbled cubes
1 tsp. coarse sea salt, or to taste
1 tsp. pepper, or more to taste
½–1½ tsp. cayenne pepper, to taste
6 lb. meat or fish
olive oil for brushing

Mix parsley, oregano, rosemary, thyme, garlic, bouillon, salt, pepper and cayenne pepper in a bowl. To determine if you wish to make mixture spicier, simply rub a little on a small piece of meat and fry it quickly in a skillet. Taste and adjust seasonings. Brush a little olive oil on meat or fish before using rub.

SEAFOOD DILL RUB

Dill is popular with fish. If using this rub for salmon, try increasing the amount of brown sugar. Turbinado sugar is similar to light brown sugar and gives the rub a crunchier crust.

3 tbs. chopped fresh dill, or 1 tbs. dried
4 tsp. paprika
1 tbs. lemon zest
2 tsp. coarse salt
1½ tsp. black pepper
1 tsp. brown or turbinado sugar, optional
½ tsp. cayenne pepper
4½ lb. seafood

Mix dill, paprika, lemon, salt, pepper, sugar and cayenne in a small bowl. Rub on fish and allow to set for 30 minutes at room temperature before grilling.

SWEET PORK RUB

This spicy rub is especially good on ribs or chops. If using barbecue sauce along with the rub, try using a sweeter sauce that has some honey or molasses added.

2½ tbs. ground allspice
2 tbs. turbinado or light brown sugar
1½ tbs. coarse salt
2 tsp.–1 tbs. chili powder, to taste
1 tbs. cinnamon
2 tsp. black pepper
1 tsp. white pepper
8 lb. pork ribs
olive oil for brushing

Mix allspice, sugar, salt, chili powder, cinnamon and black and white pepper in a small bowl. Brush meat with a little olive oil and massage in rub. Cover and refrigerate for several hours. Before grilling, remove meat from refrigerator and bring to room temperature.

SAVORY PORK RUB

Servings: ½ cup

Another version of pork rub that hasn't the sweetness or spiciness of Sweet Pork Rub, *page 36. Use with more savory sauces.*

1¾ tbs. chopped fresh thyme, or 1¾ tsp. dried
1 tbs. chopped fresh sage, or 1 tsp. dried
1 tsp. minced cloves
2 tsp. salt
1 tsp. pepper
⅓ tsp. allspice
extra virgin olive oil for rubbing
6 lb. pork

In a small bowl, combine thyme, sage, cloves, salt, pepper and allspice. Lightly oil meat with extra virgin olive oil and rub with mixture. Allow rub to infuse meat for ½ hour before grilling.

CILANTRO LAMB RUB

This is a rub reminiscent of India with a flavorful mixture of spices. One of the tricks when working with spice seeds is toasting them to enhance their flavor. Heat up a skillet on medium-high, toss in seeds and stir constantly until seeds begin to brown. Immediately remove seeds from skillet to stop the cooking process and grind with mortar and pestle or electric grinder.

¼ cup chopped fresh cilantro
2 tbs. minced fresh ginger
2 tbs. toasted cumin seeds, or 1 tbs. ground
1½ tbs. minced fresh garlic
1 tsp. chili powder
1 tsp. cinnamon
1 tsp. ground cardamom
olive oil for rubbing
8 lb. lamb or beef

Combine cilantro, ginger, cumin, garlic, chili, cinnamon and cardamom in a small bowl. Brush a little olive oil on meat and rub in spice mixture. Allow rub to set on meat for 30 minutes before grilling.

BLACKENED STEAK RUB

Blackened steak is extremely popular and several variations can be made to make it spicier or slightly sweet. If you wish the spicier mixture, add chili powder. If you want a sweeter mixture, add a small amount of turbinado or light brown sugar.

2 tbs. lemon pepper
4 tsp. paprika
1 tbs. coarse salt, or more to taste
1 tsp. dry mustard
¾ tsp. white pepper
1 pinch cayenne pepper
4 lb. steaks, beef or lamb
olive oil for rubbing

Mix pepper, paprika, salt, mustard, white pepper and cayenne in a small bowl. If you really like it extremely hot, lightly rub meat with Tabasco Sauce before massaging in rub. If you prefer a milder version, brush with olive oil and massage in rub.

JERK RUB

This is a spicy hot rub that should be used with caution. The amount of peppers will determine the heat. Use with pork, beef or chicken. This makes an all-dry rub that can be stored in a tightly sealed jar.

1/4 cup dried garlic flakes
1/4 cup onion powder
2 tbs. black pepper
2 tbs. baking soda
1 tbs. turbinado or brown sugar
2 tsp. allspice
2 tsp. ground cinnamon
2 tsp. ground nutmeg
1–2 tsp. cayenne pepper
1 tsp. dried thyme
1 tsp. dried sage
1 tsp. dried marjoram
1/4 tsp. red pepper flakes or minced
    habanero peppers, optional
8–10 lb. pork, beef, lamb or poultry

Mix all ingredients together in a bowl and store in a cool, dark place. Use sparingly as a rub. Habanero peppers are extremely hot, so be very careful not to rub your eyes after handling them.

COMPOUND BUTTERS AND BASTING SAUCES

Compound butter is a mixture of butter, herbs and spices that adds richness and extra flavor to food. Usually it is made into rolls about 2 inches in diameter and wrapped in waxed paper. It can be served chilled and cut into pats to serve on top of grilled food or cut into shapes with small cookie cutters. Compound butter can also be served melted and drizzled over food both before and after grilling or served as a dipping sauce.

HERB GARLIC BUTTER

Makes ½ cup

This compound butter can be used with all types of food including, beef, game, lamb, poultry, seafood and vegetables.

6 tbs. butter, softened
1½ tsp. minced fresh garlic
¾ tsp. black pepper
¾ tbs. minced fresh basil, or ¾ tsp. dried
½ tbs. minced fresh oregano, or ½ tsp. dried
½ tbs. minced fresh thyme leaves, or ½ tsp. dried
½ tbs. minced fresh sage, or ½ tsp. dried
⅓ tbs. minced fresh marjoram, or ⅓ tsp. dried

In a small bowl, combine softened butter with garlic, pepper, basil, oregano, thyme, sage and marjoram. Cover and chill for at least 1 hour before using.

CITRUS BUTTER

This butter makes a great accent for seafood, poultry and especially vegetables. This is also a good spread for tea breads. Cream cheese can be substituted for butter if using this recipe for bread.

$^1/_2$ cup butter, softened
$^1/_4$ cup fresh lemon juice
2 tbs. grated orange zest
$2^1/_2$ tbs. honey
1 tsp. grated lime zest
$^1/_2$ tsp. grated lemon zest

In a small bowl, combine butter, lemon juice, orange, honey, lime and lemon zest. Cover and chill for at least 1 hour before serving.

LEMON MINT BUTTER

Makes ½ cup

This is an excellent basting butter for grilled lamb and grilled vegetables. It also goes very well with cooked peas.

½ cup butter, softened
¼ cup chopped fresh mint
1 tbs. lemon juice
1 tsp. honey

In a small bowl, combine butter, mint, lemon and honey. Cover and refrigerate at least 1 hour before using.

GARLIC MUSTARD BUTTER

This is a great compound butter that enhances beef, lamb, poultry and vegetables. It also makes a good spread for sandwiches.

1 cup butter, softened
1/3 cup finely chopped parsley
1 tbs. Dijon mustard or dry mustard powder
1 tsp. minced fresh garlic
1 tsp. Worcestershire sauce
1/4 tsp. salt
1/8 tsp. pepper

Mix butter, parsley, mustard, garlic, Worcestershire sauce, salt and pepper in a bowl and stir well. Cover and refrigerate for at least 1 hour before serving.

GREEK BUTTER

I love Greek olives and this compound butter can enhance fish, poultry, beef and all kinds of vegetables. This mixture also works well as a spread for bread. If you wish to take this one step further, sprinkle with Parmesan cheese and toast under a broiler until cheese is melted.

½ cup butter, softened
¼ cup finely chopped Greek olives
1 tbs. chopped fresh rosemary, or 1 tsp. dried
1 tsp. lemon juice
1 tsp. minced fresh garlic
1 pinch black pepper

Combine butter, olives, rosemary, lemon juice, garlic and pepper in a small bowl. Cover and refrigerate for at least 1 hour before using.

TARRAGON BUTTER

Makes 1/2 cup

Tarragon has a flavor reminiscent of licorice. This recipe goes well with beef, poultry, seafood and vegetables.

1/2 cup butter, softened
2 tbs. chopped fresh tarragon, or 2 tsp. dried
1 1/2 tbs. chopped fresh parsley
1 tbs. lemon juice
3/4 tsp. salt
1/2 tsp. black pepper

In a bowl, mix together butter, tarragon, parsley, lemon juice, salt and pepper. Cover and refrigerate for at least 1 hour before using.

GORGONZOLA BUTTER

This butter is an excellent accompaniment to vegetables, chicken and beef. This may also be used as a spread for sandwiches or served as an appetizer on toasted bread rounds with cucumber or chopped fresh vegetables as a topping.

¾ cup crumbled Gorgonzola cheese
6 tbs. butter, softened
2 tbs. olive oil
1¼ tbs. chopped fresh basil, or 1¼ tsp. dried
1½ tsp. minced fresh garlic
1 tsp. lemon juice
salt and pepper to taste

In a bowl, thoroughly mix cheese, butter, olive oil, basil, garlic, lemon juice, salt and pepper. Taste and adjust seasonings. Cover and refrigerate for at least 1 hour before using.

HERB BASTING SAUCE

This is an excellent basting sauce for chicken, vegetables and seafood. This recipe can be used as a marinade for raw vegetables.

3/4 cup extra virgin olive oil
1/4 cup lemon juice or cider vinegar
1 tsp. minced fresh garlic
1/2 tsp. salt
1/8 tsp. black pepper
1/8 tsp. dried thyme
1/8 tsp. dried oregano
1 pinch dried marjoram
1/4–1/2 tsp. red pepper flakes, optional

Place olive oil, lemon juice, garlic, salt, pepper, thyme, oregano and marjoram in a food processor workbowl or blender container. Add red pepper if you wish to add a little heat to the sauce. Process until well mixed, cover and refrigerate until ready to use.

STEAK SAUCE

This potent sauce goes well with steak, hamburgers and game. If you wish to add a little heat, add a few drops of Tabasco Sauce.

3 cups dry red wine
1 cup olive oil
¾ cup finely chopped mushrooms
½ cup brandy
½ cup finely chopped fresh parsley
1 can (6 oz.) tomato paste
2–3 tsp. minced fresh garlic
½ tsp. salt
⅓ tsp. pepper
12 anchovy fillets
few drops Tabasco Sauce, optional

Place wine, oil, mushrooms, brandy, parsley, tomato paste, garlic, salt, pepper and anchovies in a food processor workbowl or blender container, and puree until smooth. Pour mixture into a saucepan, bring to a boil and reduce heat to a simmer. Simmer for 20 minutes until sauce reduces and thickens. Taste and adjust seasonings. If you wish a smooth sauce, strain through a sieve before serving.

MUSTARD SAUCE

This is an excellent sauce for steaks. Try to use fresh herbs in this recipe—they really make a difference. I have included substitutions for dried herbs if fresh herbs are not available.

½ cup Dijon mustard
1 tsp. minced fresh thyme, or ⅓ tsp. dried
1 tsp. minced fresh marjoram, or ⅓ tsp. dried
1 tsp. minced fresh parsley, or ⅓ tsp. dried
½ tsp. minced fresh rosemary, or ⅙ tsp. dried
¼ tsp. aniseed, chopped
salt and pepper to taste
¼ cup butter, softened, optional

In a bowl, thoroughly blend mustard, thyme, marjoram, parsley, rosemary, aniseed, salt and pepper. Taste and adjust seasonings. If mixture is too strong for your taste, stir in softened butter.

BARBECUE RELISH SAUCE

This sauce is generally used for hamburgers and hot dogs. It can also be used as a basting sauce for most meats, especially beef and veal.

2 tbs. olive oil
2 tbs. butter
1½ cups chopped onion
3 stalks celery, finely chopped
2 large tomatoes, deseeded, skinned and diced
1 cup ketchup
¼ cup olive oil
¼ cup balsamic vinegar
¼ cup lemon juice

¼ cup brown sugar
3 tbs. Dijon mustard
2 tbs. Worcestershire sauce
1½ tsp. salt
1 tsp. black pepper
1 pinch cayenne pepper, or few drops Tabasco Sauce
½ cup regular or sweet pickle relish, according to taste

Heat olive oil and butter in a large heavy saucepan on medium-high heat. Add onions and celery until wilted and slightly browned. Add tomatoes and cook for 5 minutes. Add ketchup, olive oil, vinegar, lemon juice, sugar, mustard, Worcestershire sauce, salt, pepper and cayenne. Cook on medium heat for 10 to 15 minutes. Taste and adjust seasoning. Place all ingredients in a food processor workbowl or blender container and puree until smooth. Stir in relish and serve.

Hint: A quick way to remove the skin from tomatoes is to plunge them into boiling water and stir for about 30 seconds, and then plunge them into ice water and immediately remove peel. The easiest way to remove seeds is to cut the tomato in half horizontally, gently squeeze it and shake out the soft insides.

LEMON CAPER SAUCE

This is a fantastic sauce for fish and vegetables. Capers add a unique piquant flavor to most dishes.

1/2 cup dry white wine
1/4 cup capers, drained
6 tbs. butter
1/3 cup lemon juice
1 1/2 tbs. finely chopped fresh parsley
1 pinch white pepper

In a small, nonaluminum saucepan, bring wine to a simmer. Add capers and simmer 3 minutes. Whisk butter in a little at a time, adding more as it is incorporated. Add lemon juice, parsley and white pepper. Taste and adjust seasonings.

SWEET ORANGE SAUCE

This is a great combination for fatty game birds like ducks and geese. Part of the recipe is for basting while cooking, and then the remaining ingredients are added and the mixture is thickened for a sauce to serve alongside.

1 cup orange juice
1 tbs. brown sugar
2 tsp. cider vinegar
2 tbs. grated orange zest
2 tbs. butter
2 tbs. flour
1 tbs. black currant jelly
1/3 cup port wine
salt and pepper to taste, optional

In a bowl, combine orange juice, brown sugar, vinegar and orange zest. Use 1/2 of this sauce to baste fowl during the grilling process. Melt butter in a small saucepan on medium-high heat and stir in flour to make a roux. Add remaining orange basting sauce to roux and stir until thickened. Stir in jelly and wine and stir again until thickened. Taste and determine if you wish to add salt and pepper. Serve this sauce alongside cooked bird.

SEAFOOD BASTING SAUCE

This makes a very quick and easy basting sauce for all types of seafood, especially salmon.

1 cup butter, melted
⅓ cup lemon juice
1½ tbs. chopped fresh parsley
2 tsp. light soy sauce
1 tsp. dried basil
1½ tsp. Worcestershire sauce
½ tsp. minced fresh garlic or garlic powder

In a small bowl, mix together butter, lemon juice, parsley, soy sauce, basil, Worcestershire sauce and garlic. Taste and adjust seasonings. Use to baste seafood while grilling.

COLA BARBECUE SAUCE

Cola gives this sauce its special flavor. This recipe works well with pork, chicken and beef. If you like your sauce less sweet, add a little more vinegar. If you prefer it sweeter, add a little more maple syrup.

1 cup cola
1 cup tomato sauce
1 can (6 oz.) tomato paste
1/2 cup Worcestershire sauce
1/2 cup molasses
1/2 cup balsamic or cider vinegar
1/2 cup brown sugar, packed
1/4 cup butter

1 tbs. Dijon mustard
1 tbs. maple syrup
1 tbs. chili powder
2 tsp. minced fresh garlic
1 tsp. savory
1 tsp. onion powder
dash Tabasco Sauce
salt and pepper to taste

Place all ingredients in a heavy saucepan. Cover pan and cook over low heat until mixture thickens, stirring occasionally.

MANGO CHUTNEY

Mango chutney is available in most grocery stores, but nothing matches chutney made from fresh ingredients. This can be served with pork, poultry, beef, fish and vegetables.

1 ½ tbs. olive oil
½ cup chopped red onions
½–1 fresh chile pepper, seeded and finely minced
1 tbs. grated fresh ginger
½ green bell pepper, seeded and finely diced

½ red bell pepper, seeded and finely diced
3 large ripe mangoes, finely diced
1 cup white wine vinegar
⅔ cup sugar
salt and black pepper to taste

Note: In this recipe, be sure to stir constantly through each of the steps until heat is set on low.

In a saucepan on medium-high heat, heat oil and sauté onions until wilted, about 6 minutes. Add ginger and chile pepper to taste. Cook for 2 minutes. Add bell peppers and cook for another 2 minutes. Reduce heat to low and add mangoes, vinegar, salt and pepper. Cook for about 15 minutes until mixture thickens, stirring occasionally at this point. Taste and adjust seasonings and remove from heat.

58   COMPOUND BUTTERS AND BASTING SAUCES

CURRIED CILANTRO MAYONNAISE

Makes 1 cup

This recipe goes well with poultry and seafood. Homemade mayonnaise is always better, but in a pinch you can substitute for the first 5 ingredients and use bottled mayonnaise instead.

2 egg yolks
1 tsp. Dijon mustard
1 tsp. lemon juice, divided
salt and white pepper to taste
1 cup extra virgin olive oil
2 tsp. finely chopped fresh cilantro
1 tsp. curry powder
$\frac{1}{2}$ tsp. minced fresh garlic

With a food processor or blender, process egg yolks, mustard, $\frac{1}{2}$ of the lemon juice, salt and pepper together until mixed. With the motor running, slowly drizzle olive oil into egg mixture until all oil is incorporated and mixture has consistency of mayonnaise. Add remaining lemon juice, cilantro, curry powder and garlic and just barely mix together. Taste and adjust seasonings.

SALADS

GRILLED VEGETABLE SALAD

Servings: 4
Grill: Hot

I love a simple salad using just fresh tomatoes, mozzarella and fresh basil leaves with no dressing. To kick it up a notch, the natural sweetness of grilled tomatoes and onions really enhances the flavor, especially with the addition of an orange juice glaze. When serving this, tell your guests that each bite should include a piece of each ingredient.

3 tbs. orange juice concentrate
2 tbs. extra virgin olive oil
1 tbs. finely chopped fresh basil
1 tsp. brown sugar
3 large tomatoes, in ½-inch slices

1 medium red onion, in ⅓-inch slices
salt and black pepper to taste
12 oz. whole milk mozzarella or
    smoked mozzarella
16 large basil leaves, or more to taste

In a bowl, mix together juice concentrate, olive oil and basil. Fire up the grill and when coals are high, brush grill rack with oil. Brush tomatoes and onion slices with orange mixture and sprinkle with salt and pepper. Grill tomatoes and onions until slightly charred and soft, about 2 to 4 minutes each side. Brush with orange mixture after turning. Cut mozzarella into ¼-inch slices and arrange on a platter alternately with tomato slices, rings of onion and basil leaves. If there is any orange dressing left, drizzle over the top.

STEAK SALAD WITH SHAVED PARMESAN

This is a popular Italian salad that is usually served with lemon wedges and large shavings of fresh Parmesan cheese. The best cheese to use is Parmigiano-Reggiano. If you wish a stronger flavor for a salad dressing I recommend a balsamic vinaigrette, Caesar dressing or a Dijon mustard dressing.

2 tsp. minced fresh garlic
3 tbs. extra virgin olive oil, divided
1 tsp. black pepper
salt to taste
3 lb. porterhouse or T-bone steak, about 1 1/2 inch
   thick
6–7 cups mixed salad greens or arugula greens,
   lightly packed
3 oz. Parmesan cheese
lemon wedges

Mash garlic with a knife until paste is formed. In a small bowl, combine mashed garlic, 1 tbs. of the olive oil, pepper and salt and stir until well combined. Pat steaks dry and smear mixture all over the meat. Cover and refrigerate at least 2 hours or up to 8 hours. Remove steaks from refrigerator 30 minutes before grilling.

Fire up the barbecue and when coals are ready, grill steaks on medium-high heat until meat is medium-rare. If available, cook steaks in a covered grill for about 4 minutes per side or until slightly pink in the center.

Cut steaks into thin slices and arrange on a plate of greens. Pour any accumulated juices from cutting the meat over the steak pieces and sprinkle with salt. Drizzle remaining oil over salad. Shave large strips of Parmesan cheese with a vegetable peeler and sprinkle over salad. Serve with lemon wedges.

MIDDLE EASTERN RICE AND LAMB SALAD

Servings: 6
Grill: Hot

This is a flavorful, spicy rice salad that goes well with tender-crisp vegetables. Beef can be substituted for lamb if desired. A nice addition is to drizzle a little extra virgin olive oil over the salad just before serving.

1 tbs. dried oregano
1 tbs. grated lemon zest
2 tsp. ground cumin
1 1/2 tsp. dried mint
3/4 tsp. coarse salt
1/2 tsp. black pepper
1 pinch garlic powder
1 1/2 lb. leg of lamb or lamb roast
1/4 cup olive oil
1 tbs. butter
3/4 cup chopped onion

1/4 cup chopped red bell pepper
2 tsp. minced fresh garlic
1 tsp. ground cumin
1 1/4 cups uncooked rice
2 1/2 cups chicken stock
1/4 cup dried currants or raisins
salt to taste
3/4 cup toasted pine nuts
1/3 cup chopped fresh mint
1 tbs. cider vinegar

In a small bowl, mix together oregano, lemon zest, cumin, mint, salt, pepper and garlic powder. Rub mixture over lamb, cover with plastic and refrigerate for 2 to 3 hours or up to 12 hours. In a heavy saucepan, heat oil and butter, add onion and red pepper, and cook for 5 minutes on medium heat. Add garlic and cook for 1 minute longer. Stir in cumin and rice and cook for 3 to 4 minutes until rice begins to look translucent. Pour in chicken stock and add currants and salt. Cover and simmer for about 18 minutes. Gently stir in pine nuts, mint and vinegar with a fork. Taste and adjust seasonings. Cover and cool while grilling meat.

Fire up the grill and when coals are hot, sear lamb for 2 to 3 minutes on each side. Reduce heat to medium and grill meat for 15 to 20 minutes, turning several times, or until cooked to medium doneness. Allow meat to cool and cut into 1/2-inch cubes. Gently stir into rice mixture and serve.

CAJUN CHICKEN SALAD

Servings: 4
Grill: Medium

This is a crisp, green salad studded with peppery chicken pieces and colorful vegetables. You can always bring up the heat by adding more Tabasco Sauce. Serve with garlic bread or crisp French bread.

2 tbs. olive oil
1 tsp. onion powder
$1/2$ tsp. black pepper
$1/4$ tsp. red pepper flakes
$1/4$ tsp. salt
1 pinch garlic powder
few drops Tabasco Sauce
4 boneless, skinless chicken breast
   halves

$1/3$ cup extra virgin olive oil
$1/4$ cup balsamic vinegar
1 tbs. sugar
$1/2$ tsp. dried thyme
$1/4$ tsp. Dijon mustard
4 cups torn mixed salad greens
$1/2$ cup thinly sliced red onion
$1/2$ red bell pepper, thinly sliced
$1/2$ cup shredded carrot

In a small bowl, combine oil, onion powder, black pepper, red pepper, salt, garlic and Tabasco Sauce. Lightly pound chicken breasts between 2 pieces of waxed paper to tenderize.

Fire up the grill and when coals are at medium, brush chicken with marinade and cook for 6 to 7 minutes per side, basting again after turning. Allow chicken to cool before slicing into small pieces. Make dressing by mixing olive oil, vinegar, sugar, thyme and mustard in a small bowl. In a salad bowl, mix together greens, red onion, bell pepper, carrot and chicken pieces. Just before serving, drizzle dressing over salad and toss to mix.

FRUITED PRAWN SALAD

Servings: 4
Grill: Medium

Frozen berries may be used in the dressing for this salad, but only use fresh berries with the greens. If using frozen berries be sure to increase sugar to taste. To make a quick vinaigrette, simply add raspberry jam to your favorite bottled oil and vinegar dressing until you get the desired flavor. Serve with warm rolls and a rich dessert.

1 lb. uncooked jumbo prawns
olive oil for brushing
1 cup fresh pea pods
salt and pepper to taste
1 cup fresh or frozen raspberries
$1/3$ cup olive oil
$1/4$ cup raspberry or white wine vinegar
1 tbs. sugar, or to taste
1 tsp. grated orange zest
$1/4$ tsp. Dijon mustard
5–6 cups torn leaf lettuce
$1/4$ small red onion, finely sliced
$1 1/2$ cups fresh raspberries

Peel, devein and butterfly prawns by making a slit along the back without cutting all the way through.

Fire up the grill, and when coals are at medium, either place prawns in a grill basket or on a mesh grill rack, or string prawns on skewers so they will not fall through the grill. Cook uncovered until prawns turn opaque, about 7 minutes, turning only once. Remove tips and strings from pea pods. Pods can be cooked like prawns by oiling lightly and using a basket or screen to grill them. Sprinkle pods with salt and pepper and cook for 3 to 5 minutes. If you prefer, pods can be cooked in boiling water for about 3 minutes or until tender-crisp, rinsed in cold water, drained and set aside.

With a food processor or blender, puree raspberries, olive oil, raspberry vinegar, sugar, orange zest and Dijon mustard. Taste and adjust seasonings. Arrange lettuce on 4 individual plates, divide pea pods and prawns among plates and sprinkle with red onions and raspberries. Serve dressing alongside.

SWEET POTATO SALAD

This is similar to German potato salad but uses grilled sweet potatoes instead. This dish would go well with grilled steak and steamed greens or asparagus.

1/2 tsp. salt
5 medium sweet potatoes or yams, peeled
1/4 cup olive oil
salt and pepper to taste
1/2 lb. bacon
1 large red onion, chopped
1–1 1/2 tbs. minced fresh garlic, to taste
3/4 cup cider vinegar
1/2 cup olive oil
1/3 cup sugar
1/2 cup chopped fresh parsley

Fill a large saucepan ⅔ full of water, add salt and bring to a boil. Cut yams into 1-inch rounds and cook in salted water until just fork-tender, about 8 minutes. Do not overcook, or slices will be too mushy to grill. Drain and set aside to cool. Mix oil with salt and pepper in a large bowl and toss with sweet potatoes until completely covered.

Fire up the grill and heat coals to medium-hot. Grill sweet potato slices for about 4 minutes, turning only once, until well browned. Remove potatoes from heat and set aside in a salad bowl. Dice bacon and cook over medium-high heat in a medium skillet until brown and crisp. Drain bacon on paper towels and add to sweet potato slices. Reserve about 2 tbs. rendered fat and discard the rest. Cook red onions on medium for 3 minutes. Add garlic and cook for 1 minute longer, until garlic is wilted but not browned. Remove skillet from stove and add vinegar, olive oil and sugar. Stir to combine. Pour mixture over sweet potatoes. Add parsley, salt and pepper. Taste, adjust seasonings and serve.

BLACKENED BEEF SALAD

Cold, crisp greens are a perfect complement to spicy meat. Grilled potatoes and vegetables make a good accompaniment to this salad. I would suggest a fruit dessert.

2 tbs. paprika
4 tsp. black pepper
2–3 tsp. salt
$1\frac{3}{4}$ tsp. garlic powder
$1\frac{1}{2}$ tsp. cayenne powder
1 tsp. dried oregano
1 tsp. dried thyme
6 tbs. butter, melted
$1\frac{1}{2}$ lb. beef tenderloin steaks, $\frac{1}{2}$-inch thick
10–12 cups mixed greens

1 cup thinly sliced red onion
2 tomatoes, in wedges
$\frac{3}{4}$ cup black or Greek olives
$\frac{3}{4}$ cup sliced yellow or green bell pepper
6 oz. crumbled blue cheese
$\frac{1}{2}$ cup extra virgin olive oil
3 tbs. balsamic vinegar
$\frac{1}{2}$ tsp. Dijon mustard
1 pinch sugar
salt and pepper to taste

In a small bowl, combine paprika, black pepper, salt, garlic powder, cayenne pepper, oregano and thyme. Brush steaks with melted butter and sprinkle with rub mixture. Let steaks set at room temperature for 1/2 hour before grilling.

Fire up the grill and when coals are very hot, grill steaks, about 2 minutes per side for medium-rare or to the desired doneness. Allow meat to set for a few minutes before slicing into thin strips. In a salad bowl, mix together greens, red onions, tomatoes, olives and peppers. Lay strips of grilled meat on top and sprinkle with blue cheese.

In a small bowl, combine olive oil, vinegar, mustard, sugar, salt and pepper. Taste and adjust seasonings. Serve dressing alongside salad.

GREEK PRAWN SALAD

Servings: 4
Grill: Medium-hot

Adding grilled prawns to this popular salad makes it a refreshing entrée. Serve with hot pita bread or a crusty French bread and a fruit dessert. Try to find Greek oregano if possible, as it has a stronger flavor with a peppery taste. To add beautiful color to your salad, use all three colors of peppers.

1/4 cup extra virgin olive oil or Greek olive oil, divided
1/4 cup lemon juice, divided
2 tsp. chopped fresh oregano, or 2/3 tsp. dried, divided
1/2 tsp. minced fresh garlic, divided
salt and black pepper to taste
1/2 English cucumber
1 pint cherry tomatoes
1/2 cup thinly sliced red onions
1 cup cubed green, yellow or red bell peppers, 1-inch cubes
1 lb. (24 per lb.) prawns, shelled and deveined
bamboo skewers, soaked in water for 1/2 hour
1/2 lb. feta cheese, in 1/2-inch dice
1 cup Greek olives

74   SALADS

In a nonaluminum bowl, mix together 3 tbs. of the olive oil, $\frac{1}{2}$ of the lemon juice, 1 tsp. of the oregano, $\frac{1}{4}$ tsp. of the garlic, and salt and pepper to taste. Cut cucumbers into 1-inch chunks and add to dressing with tomatoes, red onion and peppers. In a separate bowl, mix remaining tbs. olive oil, lemon juice, oregano and garlic together and add prawns. Marinate prawns for 15 minutes before grilling. Thread prawns onto bamboo skewers and sprinkle with salt and pepper.

Fire up the grill and when coals are medium-hot, place skewers on grill and cook for about 2 minutes per side or until prawns turn pink and meat is opaque. Add grilled prawns to marinating vegetables along with feta cheese and olives.

MANGO CHICKEN SALAD

This is an Asian version of chicken salad with fruit, strong herbs and a citrus dressing. Serve with hot bread and maybe a chocolate or custard dessert.

4 boneless, skinless chicken breast
   halves
2 tbs. extra virgin olive oil
salt and pepper to taste
1 pinch cayenne pepper
2 ripe mangoes, peeled, in $1/2$-inch dice
$1 1/2$ cups mixed red and green seedless
   grapes, halved
$1/2$ cup diced red onion
$1/2$ red bell pepper, in $1/2$-inch dice
3 tbs. chopped fresh cilantro

2 tbs. chopped fresh basil
$1/2$ cup orange juice
$1/4$ cup lime juice
2 tbs. extra virgin olive oil
1 tbs. grated fresh ginger
1 tbs. grated lime zest
salt and black pepper to taste
dash Tabasco Sauce, or more to taste
$1/2$ cup toasted almonds, peanuts or
   walnuts, optional
mint sprigs for garnish

Brush chicken breast with olive oil and sprinkle with salt, pepper and cayenne. Fire up the grill and when coals are medium-hot, cook chicken for about 7 minutes per side. Meat should be opaque inside with no pink color remaining. Remove from grill and allow chicken to cool to room temperature. Cut chicken into $\frac{1}{2}$-inch cubes and place in a bowl with mangoes, grapes, onions, bell peppers, cilantro and basil.

Make the dressing: In a bowl, whisk together orange juice, lime juice, olive oil, ginger, lime zest, salt, pepper and Tabasco Sauce. Pour over chicken mixture, cover and refrigerate for at least 30 minutes before serving. Just before serving, add toasted nuts and garnish with sprigs of mint.

GRILLED NEW POTATO SALAD

This is a new twist to the standard American salad. It can be served hot or cold and goes extremely well with beef and poultry dishes. Yukon golds are my favorite potatoes to cook with because they have a lot of protein, a lot of flavor and a rich, yellow color.

16 small new potatoes
2 qt. salted water
olive oil
coarse sea salt or seasoning salt to taste
black pepper to taste
bamboo skewers, soaked in water for 20 minutes
$1/3$ cup extra virgin olive oil
2 tbs. fresh lemon juice
1 tbs. Dijon mustard, or more to taste
$1/4$ cup finely minced fresh parsley
2–3 tsp. finely minced fresh garlic
several dashes Tabasco Sauce, or more to taste
1 pinch cayenne pepper, or more to taste

In a large saucepan, cook potatoes in boiling salted water until just barely cooked and still firm, about 15 minutes. Immediately drain and rinse in cold water to stop the cooking process. If you have a grill basket or mesh screen, use this to cook potatoes on grill, or you will have to thread potatoes onto bamboo skewers to keep them from falling through grill. Cut potatoes in half, brush with olive oil and sprinkle with coarse salt and pepper. Thread onto bamboo skewers.

Fire up the grill and when coals are medium-hot, cook until golden brown, about 5 minutes. When done, remove potatoes from skewers and mix with lemon juice, mustard, parsley, garlic, Tabasco Sauce and cayenne pepper. Taste and adjust seasonings. Allow flavors to blend for at least 1 hour before serving.

Hint: Use regular olive oil to cook with because it has a higher burning point than extra virgin olive oil. Extra virgin has more flavor, so it is generally used in dressings.

BEEF, LAMB AND PORK

LEMON HERB LAMB CHOPS

Servings: 6
Grill: Medium-hot

Lamb chops are grilled and served with a pungent lemon herb mixture. This would go well with a chopped vegetable or Greek salad and crusty bread. Using fresh herbs makes a big difference but in case fresh herbs are not available I've given the dried herb amounts.

2½ tbs. chopped fresh oregano, or
  2½ tsp. dried
2½ tbs. chopped fresh thyme, or
  2½ tsp. dried
2½ tbs. lemon juice
1½ tbs. grated lemon zest, or
  1¼ tsp. dried

1½ tsp. salt
pepper to taste
1 pinch sugar
½ cup extra virgin olive oil
6 shoulder blade lamb chops, ¾-inch
  thick
salt and pepper for seasoning

With a blender, food processor or mortar and pestle, grind together oregano and thyme; add lemon juice, zest, salt, pepper and sugar. Continue to grind until a paste is formed. Add oil in a fine stream or, if mixing by hand, add a small amount at a time, whisking until all oil is incorporated and emulsified. Taste and adjust seasonings and set aside. Season lamb chops with salt and pepper. Fire up the grill and when coals are medium-hot, brush grill with a little olive oil and grill chops. Cook for about 4 minutes each side for medium-rare, turning only once. Serve with sauce alongside.

BEEF FAJITA

Servings: 6
Grill: Medium-hot

For the best flavor, beef should be marinated for at least 24 hours. Marinating beef in lime juice tenderizes the meat. Serve with grilled vegetables, refried beans, guacamole, sour cream and salsa.

$1/3$ cup olive oil
$1/3$ cup lime juice
3 tbs. chopped fresh cilantro
1 tbs. chopped onion
2 tsp. minced fresh garlic
$1^1/2$ tsp. crushed red pepper
$1/3$ tsp. salt
$1/3$ tsp. black pepper
2 lb. skirt steak, trimmed of excess fat
12 medium flour tortillas
grilled onions and bell peppers, guacamole, salsa, refried beans, chopped
    tomatoes, chopped lettuce and shredded cheese, optional

82   BEEF, LAMB AND PORK

Mix together olive oil, lime juice, cilantro, onion, garlic, red pepper, salt and pepper in a shallow, nonaluminum baking dish. Tenderize meat by pounding with a mallet for about 30 seconds on each side. Place meat in marinade, cover and refrigerate for at least 24 hours.

Fire up the grill and add soaked mesquite chips, if desired. Sprinkle tortillas with a little water, wrap in aluminum foil and place in warming rack or cool part of the grill (turn halfway through grilling). When coals are medium-hot, brush oil on the grill rack; place meat on grill and brush with marinade. Cover and cook until meat is medium-well done, about 4 to 5 minutes per side depending on thickness of meat. When you turn meat, baste again with marinade. Remove meat from grill and slice into thin strips. Serve with warmed tortillas, grilled onions and bell peppers, guacamole, salsa, refried beans and, if desired, chopped tomatoes, chopped lettuce and shredded cheese.

WINE-MARINATED BEEF TENDERLOIN

Servings: 6
Grill: Medium-hot

Wine tenderizes meat as well as adding flavor. I like to use Pinot Noir or Zinfandel. This grilled tenderloin would go well with tarragon butter.

1 1/2 cups dry red wine
1/2 cup extra virgin olive oil
1/3 cup red wine or balsamic vinegar
1/2 cup chopped onion
1/2 cup chopped carrot

1 pinch crushed bay leaves
3/4 tsp. black pepper
4 lb. trimmed beef tenderloin
olive oil for brushing

With a blender or food processor, puree together wine, oil, vinegar, onion, carrot, crushed bay leaf and black pepper. Pour into a locking plastic bag, add beef tenderloin and massage well to distribute marinade. About 30 minutes before grilling, remove meat from marinade and pat dry. Refrigerate for several hours before grilling. Fire up the grill, and when coals are medium-hot brush grill with olive oil; place meat on rack and brown on all sides. Reduce heat to medium (close grill cover and open vents half way). Cook until meat registers 140° on the thermometer for medium-rare, or to desired doneness. Allow meat to rest for 10 minutes before carving.

MIXED SAUSAGE BARBECUE

Servings: 6
Grill: Medium

Start out with good quality sausages or hot dogs for the perfect grill. Try mild and spicy Italian links, bratwurst, andouille sausage, Portuguese linguica, knockwurst, bockwurst, Louisiana links and hot dogs (hot and mild varieties). Be sure to include a large assortment of condiments to satisfy everyone's taste. This grill would go well with a tossed green salad and potato casserole. The sausages are generally eaten without bread, but I like to give my guests the option, so I generally include lightly buttered, toasted rolls or buns.

olive oil for brushing	sauerkraut
12–18 assorted sausages and hot dogs	chopped sautéed onions
rolls or buns, optional	ketchup
butter for bread	mayonnaise
prepared mustard assortment	relish

Separate sausage links and prick skin in several places with a fork. Fire up the grill, and when coals are at medium, brush rack with oil and place sausages on grill. Turn frequently to brown on all sides. Cook for about 15 minutes or until no pink remains in the meat. Be careful of flare-ups from grease—keep a water bottle handy. Brush bread with butter and either toast under a broiler or cook on grill until light brown. Serve grilled meats immediately with bread and condiments listed.

BABY BACK RIBS

Servings: 6-8
Grill: Medium-hot

Baby backs are the tender little bones that run alongside the pork loin. These ribs are cooked entirely on the grill with indirect heat so the ribs take on a smoky flavor.

1/4 cup butter
1 1/4 cups chopped onions
1 cup ketchup
1 cup dark molasses
1 cup brown sugar, packed
1 cup water
1 cup bottled chili sauce
1/2 cup cider vinegar
1/4 cup Worcestershire sauce
1/4 cup lemon juice
1 tbs. Dijon mustard
1 tsp. paprika
1 tsp. black pepper
1/2 tsp. liquid smoke, or more to taste
6–8 lb. pork baby back ribs

In a heavy saucepan, heat butter, add onions and cook over medium heat until onions are wilted. Add ketchup, molasses, brown sugar, water, chili sauce, vinegar, Worcestershire sauce, lemon juice, mustard, paprika, pepper and liquid smoke. Simmer on medium heat, uncovered, for $\frac{1}{2}$ hour or until mixture thickens to sauce consistency. Place an aluminum drip pan in center of grill under rack and surround with coals.

Fire up grill and when coals are medium-hot, brush with oil and place ribs meat-side-up on the grill. Spread ribs with barbecue sauce and cover with hood, adjusting vents for even heat. Cook for 1 to $1\frac{1}{4}$ hours or until meat is no longer pink. Turn occasionally and baste with sauce each time. Heat remaining sauce and serve alongside ribs.

MEXI-BURGER

Serve this with guacamole and salsa or sliced tomatoes. Other condiments could be sliced olives, mild green chiles, a sprinkling of jalapeños or lettuce.

2½ lb. lean ground beef
½ cup finely chopped onion
¼ cup bottled taco sauce
2 tsp. dried oregano
2 tsp. chili powder
1½ tsp. minced fresh garlic
1 tsp. ground cumin
1 tsp. salt
1 pinch pepper
8–10 slices medium cheddar or Monterey jack cheese
⅓ cup butter, melted
½ tsp. chili powder
¼ tsp. barbecue spice, optional
8–10 rolls or buns

In a large bowl, mix together beef, onion, taco sauce, oregano, 2 tsp. of the chili powder, garlic, cumin, salt and pepper. Form meat mixture into 8 or 10 patties.

Fire up the grill and when coals are at medium, brush rack with oil and place patties on grill. Cook for about 5 to 7 minutes per side, depending on desired level of doneness. I like to cover grill to give burgers a stronger smoky flavor. Just before serving, place cheese on meat and cook until cheese just begins to melt. In a small bowl, combine butter with chili powder and barbecue spice. Brush on bread, place on grill and cook until just lightly toasted. Serve immediately with meat patties and condiments.

DRY RUB T-BONE STEAK

Servings: 4
Grill: Hot

This simple rub adds a lot of flavor to the steak. Serve with a flavored butter for extra richness. A crisp green salad and garlic bread or potatoes goes well with this.

3 tbs. dried basil
1 1/4 tbs. dried sage
2–3 tsp. coarse salt
1 tsp. black pepper
4 T-bone steaks, about 1 1/4-inch thick, 1 lb. each
6 tbs. unsalted butter
2 tbs. extra virgin olive oil
3 tbs. chopped fresh basil, or 1 tbs. dried
2 1/2 tbs. chopped fresh sage,
    or 2 1/2 tsp. dried
1 tsp. anchovy paste
1 pinch white pepper

In a small bowl, combine basil, sage, salt and pepper. Massage rub mixture into steaks. Cover and refrigerate for at least 2 hours. Remove steaks from refrigerator ½ hour before grilling.

Fire up the grill and when coals are hot, brush rack with oil and sear steaks for 2 to 3 minutes on each side. Reduce heat to medium or move steaks to a cooler section of grill. Cook 2 to 3 minutes longer, turning several times. Cover grill and cook for about 5 minutes, or until desired doneness. In a bowl, combine butter, olive oil, basil, sage, anchovy paste and white pepper. Serve grilled steak with a small amount of flavored butter.

PEACHY RIBS

Servings: 4
Grill: Medium

This very simple, sweet glaze packs a lot of flavor and really compliments the ribs. A good accompaniment would be grilled asparagus and a potato casserole.

4 lb. spareribs
coarse salt and black pepper to taste
oil for brushing grill
1 jar (10 oz.) peach preserves

$2\frac{1}{2}$ tbs. fresh lemon juice
1 tbs. water
1 tsp. Dijon mustard
1 pinch white pepper

Place an aluminum drip pan under rack and surround pan with coals. Fire up the grill and when coals are at medium, brush grill with oil. Remove excess fat from ribs. Sprinkle with salt and pepper and place ribs over drip pan. Cover grill and cook for $1\frac{1}{2}$ hours until ribs are tender and no pink remains in meat. With a food processor or blender, puree preserve until smooth. Pour pureed preserves into a small saucepan; add lemon juice, water, mustard and white pepper. Stir to combine. Cook on medium heat until mixture melts and becomes thin enough to brush. Brush on ribs in the last 15 minutes of cooking. Serve immediately.

ROSEMARY LAMB CHOPS

Servings: 6
Grill: Medium

For this dish, lamb chops are marinated in a wine and rosemary mixture and grilled to perfection. Sometimes I like to sprinkle a little shredded Parmesan cheese on the chops just before serving. For extra flavor, serve some mint jelly on the side.

$1/2$ cup dry white wine
$1/2$ cup lemon juice
$1/3$ cup finely chopped onion
$1/4$ cup extra virgin olive oil
$1 1/4$ tbs. chopped fresh rosemary, or
  $1 1/4$ tsp. dried

1 tsp. minced fresh garlic
1 tsp. sugar
$3/4$ tsp. salt
$1/3$ tsp. black pepper
12 lamb loin chops, about 1 inch thick

In a nonaluminum bowl, mix together wine, lemon juice, onion, oil, rosemary, garlic, sugar, salt and pepper and pour into a locking plastic bag. Trim excess fat from chops and add them to bag. Seal and massage bag to distribute marinade and refrigerate overnight. Remove meat from marinade and bring chops to room temperature, about $1/2$ hour. Place an aluminum drip pan under grill and surround with coals. Fire up grill and when coals are at medium, brush rack with oil and place chops over drip pan. Cover and cook for 15 to 20 minutes, brushing with marinade when turning.

HAM AND PORK PATTIES

When you are tired of ordinary beef burgers, try this alternative. It is reminiscent of meat loaf but with a semi-sweet glaze. Serve with buns, lettuce and mayonnaise.

1 1/2 cups soft breadcrumbs
1/4 cup milk
1/3 cup chopped onion, or more to taste
2 beaten eggs
1 1/2 tsp. commercially prepared
    horseradish sauce
1/8 tsp. black pepper

1 lb. lean ground pork
1 lb. ground cooked ham
1/2 cup red currant jelly
1/3 cup ketchup
2 tsp. Worcestershire sauce
2 tsp. Dijon mustard

In a large bowl, combine breadcrumbs with milk and let sit for 5 minutes. Add onions, eggs, horseradish and pepper and stir to combine. Add pork and ham and mix well. Make a small patty and fry it. Taste and adjust seasonings. Shape adjusted mixture into patties. In a small saucepan, combine jelly, ketchup, Worcestershire sauce and mustard and cook on medium heat until jelly melts. Keep glaze warm until ready to serve. Fire up the grill and when coals are at medium, brush rack with oil and cook patties for about 15 minutes until juices run clear, turning once. Just before serving, brush glaze on top. Serve remaining glaze alongside.

PARMESAN BASIL BURGERS

Servings: 8
Grill: Medium

Basil is one of my favorite herbs. Try to use fresh basil whenever possible. The meat is a combination of beef and turkey, but any ground meat combination will work: beef and veal, chicken and turkey, pork and beef, etc. Serve with toasted buns, mayonnaise, tomato slices, lettuce and condiments.

3/4 cup chopped onion
3/4 cup grated Parmesan cheese
3 tbs. chopped fresh basil, or 1 tbs. dried
1/4 cup ketchup

1 tsp. minced fresh garlic
1/4 tsp. salt
1/3 tsp. black pepper, or to taste
1 lb. lean ground beef or ground chuck
1 lb. ground turkey

In a large bowl, thoroughly mix onion, cheese, basil, ketchup, garlic, salt and pepper. Add meats and stir well to combine. Make a small patty, fry it in a skillet, taste and adjust seasonings. Form remaining mixture into large patties. Fire up the grill and when coals are at medium, brush a little oil on rack and place patties on grill. Cook for about 15 minutes, turning only once. Meat should not have any pink color remaining inside. Serve immediately.

PORK CHOPS WITH RUM BBQ SAUCE

Servings: 4
Grill: Hot

This is a luscious sauce with a sweet and spicy flavor. A good accompaniment would be either applesauce or grilled fruit. This sauce also goes well with grilled chicken.

1 tbs. olive oil
1 tbs. butter
1 cup chopped onion
2 tbs. grated fresh ginger
1 1/2 tbs. minced fresh garlic
1 cup dark rum
1 cup ketchup
1/2 cup balsamic vinegar

1/2 cup molasses or honey
1/4 cup brown sugar, packed
2 1/2 tsp. allspice
1/8 tsp. mace or nutmeg
salt and black pepper to taste
4 extra-thick pork loin chops
olive oil for brushing
coarse salt and black pepper to taste

In a heavy saucepan, heat oil and butter on medium-high heat until butter is melted. Add onion and cook until onion is wilted, about 5 minutes. Add ginger and garlic and stir for 1 minute. Add rum, ketchup, vinegar, molasses, sugar, allspice, mace, salt and pepper and bring to a boil. Immediately reduce temperature and simmer for 15 to 20 minutes. Remove from heat, taste and adjust seasonings. Trim any excess fat from chops, lightly brush with oil and sprinkle with salt and pepper.

Fire up the grill and when coals are hot, brush rack with oil. Quickly sear chops for 3 to 4 minutes per side. Reduce heat to medium-low and cook for about 10 minutes per side. Meat should not have any pink color remaining. Brush on sauce just before serving. Serve remaining sauce along with grilled chops.

ISLAND BURGERS

Servings: 4
Grill: Medium-hot

For a change, these burgers are made with pork, but ground beef, veal, chicken, or turkey can be substituted. Grilled sweet onions really make this burger special. If Walla Walla sweet onions or Vidalia onions are available, use in place of red onions.

1 1/2 lb. lean ground pork
1/2 cup breadcrumbs
3 tbs. dry white wine
3–4 tsp. curry powder
1 tbs. grated fresh ginger
2 tsp. minced fresh garlic
1 tsp. salt
1/2 tsp. allspice
several dashes Tabasco Sauce

1/4 cup mayonnaise
1/3 cup diced mango
1 tbs. lime juice
1 tsp. honey
4 thick slices red onion
butter for brushing
4 hamburger buns or sourdough rolls
lettuce for garnish

In a bowl, combine pork, bread, wine, curry powder, ginger, garlic, salt and all-spice. In a skillet, fry a small patty, taste and adjust seasonings. Form meat mixture into 4 patties. With a blender or food processor, mix together mayonnaise, mango, lime juice and honey.

Fire up the grill and when coals are medium-hot, brush rack with oil and place patties on grill. Cover and grill for about 5 to 6 minutes per side. While patties are cooking, brush onion slices with butter and place on rack. Cook for about 2 minutes per side or until tender-crisp and brown. Brush buns with butter and toast on grill. Assemble burgers with toasted buns, mango mayonnaise, pork patties and lettuce.

Note: If you prefer a less sweet burger, use regular mayonnaise in place of mango mayonnaise.

LAMB SHISH KEBAB

Servings: 4
Grill: Medium-hot

What's a barbecue book without a shish kebab! Possible accompaniments with this meal would be pasta and a fruited green salad. Feel free to vary the vegetables.

1/4 cup extra virgin olive oil
3 tbs. chopped fresh cilantro
1 tsp. paprika
1 tsp. ground cumin
3/4 tsp. black pepper, or more to taste
2 tsp. minced fresh garlic
1 1/2 lb. boneless lamb leg, in 1-inch cubes
1/2 lb. meaty smoked bacon or smoked ham, in 1-inch cubes
2 portobello mushrooms, quartered, or 8 whole white mushrooms
8 very small peeled onions or
    2 medium onions, quartered
8 pieces fresh or canned pineapple cubes
2 red, green or yellow bell peppers
    in 1-inch squares
melted butter

In a bowl, mix together olive oil, cilantro, paprika, cumin, pepper and garlic. Rub into lamb cubes and let sit for 1 hour. Thread remaining ingredients along with meat onto 4 skewers, alternating ingredients. If bacon seems too fatty, precook in a skillet until most of the fat is rendered.

Fire up the grill and when coals are medium-hot, brush rack with oil and place kebabs over coals. Brush a little melted butter on vegetables and grill for about 6 to 8 minutes, until meat is medium-rare, or to desired doneness.

STEAK WITH GREEN SALSA

Servings: 4
Grill: Hot

Fresh green salsa is the perfect complement to succulent tenderloin steak. A good accompaniment would be stuffed broiled tomatoes and baked or grilled potatoes.

2/3 cup extra virgin olive oil
1/2 cup chopped fresh parsley or cilantro, packed
12 whole basil leaves
10 fresh mint leaves
1 tbs. capers, drained
2 tsp. Dijon mustard
1 1/2 tsp. anchovy paste
1/2 tsp. balsamic vinegar
1/2 tsp. minced fresh garlic
salt and black pepper to taste
4 tenderloin steaks, 2 inches thick, 6 oz. each
kitchen string
olive oil for brushing
black pepper for rubbing

With a food processor or blender, puree extra virgin olive oil, parsley, basil, mint, capers, mustard, anchovy paste, vinegar, garlic, salt and pepper until well combined. Tie kitchen string around steaks to hold their shape. Brush steaks with olive oil and rub in black pepper.

Fire up the grill and when coals are hot, grill each side for 3 to 6 minutes depending on desired doneness (3 minutes for rare and 6 minutes for well-done). Remove steaks from grill, remove string, salt and serve topped with green salsa.

POULTRY

CHICKEN WITH MINT CHUTNEY

Servings: 6
Grill: Medium-hot

This chutney is highly flavored with a mixture of mint and orange and can be mild or hot depending on the amount of chiles used. Make the sauce just before serving, or the mint will darken.

2 cups fresh mint leaves
1/3 cup chopped red onion
1/4 cup water
3 tbs. lime juice
1 1/2 tbs. orange juice
1 1/2 tbs. sugar
1 tbs. orange zest

1 tsp.–1 tbs. chopped, seeded red chiles
  or green jalapeño chiles, optional
salt to taste
2 tbs. olive oil for brushing
2 tbs. lime juice
6 boneless, skinless chicken breast
  halves
salt and pepper to taste

With a food processor or blender, blend mint leaves, onion, water, lime juice, orange juice, sugar, orange zest, chiles and salt until leaves are coarsely chopped. Fire up the grill and heat coals to medium-hot. Mix 2 tbs. olive oil and 2 tbs. lime juice and brush mixture on chicken breasts. Sprinkle each breast with salt and pepper and place on grill about 6 inches from coals. Cook for 4 to 5 minutes on each side until just cooked through. Spread some mint mixture on chicken and serve remaining sauce alongside.

CHICKEN FAJITAS

I like to use mesquite wood chips when grilling this chicken recipe. Serve with tortillas, guacamole, sour cream, grilled vegetables and salsa. If desired, also include shredded cheeses, chopped tomatoes and finely chopped lettuce.

1/3 cup fresh lime juice
3 tbs. olive oil
3/4 cup tequila, dry white wine or orange juice
3/4 cup chopped onion
1/4 cup chopped fresh cilantro
salt and pepper to taste
6 boneless, skinless chicken breast halves
12 small flour or corn tortillas

Combine lime juice, oil, tequila, onions, cilantro, salt and pepper in a shallow, nonaluminum baking dish. With a sharp knife, cut criss-cross slits in chicken breast about $1/2$-inch wide and $1/4$-inch deep. This will allow marinade to permeate meat better.

Place chicken breasts in marinade, cover and refrigerate for 2 to 3 hours or overnight. Remove marinated chicken from refrigerator 30 minutes before grilling. Fire up the grill and sprinkle soaked mesquite chips, if available, evenly over the coals.

Lightly moisten tortillas with water and wrap with aluminum. Place packet on warming rack or the coolest part of grill. Turn packet halfway through grilling process. When grill is medium-hot, place chicken on rack, baste with marinade, cover and cook for about 3 to 4 minutes. Turn and baste 3 more times for a total cooking time of 12 to 16 minutes or until chicken meat is slightly firm to the touch or meat is opaque throughout. Thinly slice chicken and serve with warm tortillas.

BEER CHICKEN

A whole chicken is roasted upright set on an open can of beer. The beer tenderizes and adds moisture resulting in very succulent meat. The chicken does not take on a beer flavor though. It is very important that you have a level barbecue. If barbecue has a hanging rack, remove it so it won't knock bird over when you open the grill. Trust me—I learned this from experience! You might need to have a few extra cans of beer on hand in case bird topples over.

4½–5 lb. whole roasting chicken
salt and pepper to taste
1 tbs. olive oil

1 tbs. chopped fresh rosemary, or
  1 tsp. dried
1 can (12 oz.) beer

Rinse chicken inside and out with cold running water. Pat dry with paper towels and sprinkle salt and pepper in main and neck cavities. Rub olive oil on outside of bird and sprinkle rosemary and more pepper. Open beer can and insert it in main cavity of bird so chicken will be setting upright on can. Use the indirect grilling method: place a shallow aluminum pan in center of coals so fat drippings won't create flames that will over-char chicken. Fire up the grill and when coals are medium-hot, carefully place chicken on grill over pan and cover. Check occasionally, being very careful not to upset the bird when opening grill. Barbecue for about 55 minutes, until a thermometer registers 165° or liquid runs clear when piercing the drumstick.

LEMON CHICKEN

This is a very easy recipe that should be made a day ahead of time so marinade can infuse chicken with flavor. Serve with fruited green salad and potatoes or rice pilaf. When cooking chicken, use tongs to turn so skin is not pierced with a fork.

$^1/_2$ cup mayonnaise
$^1/_4$ cup lemon juice
1 tbs. finely grated lemon zest
1 tbs. chopped fresh basil, or 1 tsp. dried
1 tbs. finely minced onion

$1^1/_2$ tsp. salt
1 tsp. minced fresh garlic
$^1/_2$ tsp. paprika
$^1/_4$ tsp. dried thyme
1 fryer chicken, $4^1/_2$ lb.

In a small bowl, combine mayonnaise, lemon juice, lemon zest, basil, onion, salt, garlic, paprika and thyme. Cut chicken in half and place in a glass or nonaluminum pan. Spread marinade over chicken halves, cover with plastic wrap and refrigerate overnight, turning occasionally. Place an aluminum drip pan under grill and surround with coals. Fire up the grill and when coals are medium-hot, set chicken halves skin-side-up on grill over pan. Cover grill and cook for 30 minutes, basting frequently with marinade. Turn, baste and continue to cook until chicken is golden brown and drumstick will move easily when shaken, about 15 to 20 minutes longer.

TANDOORI CHICKEN BREAST

Servings: 4-6
Grill: Medium-hot

Tandoori is a popular dish from India where the meat is tenderized in a spicy yogurt marinade. Serve with a tossed salad and fresh hot bread like Indian naan bread.

1 cup plain yogurt
2 tbs. lemon juice
1 tbs. fresh grated ginger
1 tsp. ground cumin
1 tsp. sugar
$1/2$ tsp. ground coriander
1 tsp. minced fresh garlic
$1/2$ tsp. turmeric
$1/4$ tsp. salt
$1/8$ tsp. red pepper flakes
8 boneless, skinless chicken breast halves
thinly sliced onions and chopped tomato for garnish

In a bowl, combine yogurt, lemon juice, ginger, cumin, sugar, coriander, garlic, turmeric, salt and red pepper flakes. Cut 3 to 4 slits ⅛-inch deep into each chicken breast. Place marinade and chicken in a large locking plastic bag, massage bag to thoroughly coat chicken and refrigerate for at least 8 hours, but ideally 24 hours. Remove chicken from refrigerator 30 minutes before grilling. Place an aluminum drip pan under the grill and surround with coals.

Fire up grill and when coals reach medium-hot, place chicken on grill, baste with a little marinade, cover and cook for about 20 minutes or until chicken is tender and no pink remains. Baste with marinade each time you turn chicken.

SESAME CHICKEN

Servings: 4
Grill: Medium-hot

It is important to the flavor of this recipe to use soaked mesquite wood chips. Serve as an entrée or as part of a delicious salad with sesame oil dressing.

1/4 cup peanut oil
1/3 cup rice vinegar
3 tbs. light soy sauce
1 1/2 tbs. toasted sesame seeds
2 tbs. finely minced green onions
1 tbs. chopped fresh ginger
1 tbs. toasted sesame oil
few dashes red chili oil to taste
4 chicken breast halves with skin

In a small bowl, mix oil, vinegar, soy sauce, sesame seeds, green onions, ginger, sesame oil and chili oil. Pour into a locking plastic bag with chicken. Seal and massage bag to distribute marinade. Refrigerate for several hours, massaging bag occasionally. Place an aluminum drip pan in center of grill under rack. Pile coals around outside of pan.

Fire up the grill and when coals are medium-hot, add soaked mesquite chips. Remove chicken from refrigerator. Drain off marinade and reserve for basting. Place chicken skin-side down over hot coals to sear in juices. Cook for about 4 minutes each side, watching carefully to avoid flare-ups. Move chicken to area above drip pan, baste with marinade, cover grill and check about every 5 minutes. Turn and baste each time you check until chicken is browned and color of meat is opaque with no pink remaining, about 15 to 20 minutes longer.

GINGER CHICKEN WINGS

Servings: 4
Grill: Medium

This recipe is served as an entrée with the whole wing intact. It can also be served as an appetizer by dividing wing into little drumettes. This would go well with a potato casserole, grilled potatoes or rice pilaf and green vegetables.

1/2 cup soy sauce
2 tbs. extra virgin olive oil
2 tbs. brown sugar
2 tbs. lemon juice or rice wine vinegar
1 1/2 tbs. finely minced green onions

2 tsp. grated fresh ginger
1/2 tsp. minced fresh garlic
1/4 tsp. pepper
4 lb. chicken wings

In a bowl, combine soy sauce, oil, sugar, lemon juice, green onions, ginger, garlic and pepper. Transfer to a locking plastic bag. Rinse chicken under cold running water and pat dry. If there are hairs on the skin, burn them off with a candle. Toss chicken in bag with marinade, seal and refrigerate for several hours before grilling. Fire up the grill and when coals are at medium, brush grill with a little oil and place chicken on rack. Cook, turning occasionally, for about 20 minutes or until meat is no longer pink.

MAPLE CHICKEN

Servings: 6
Grill: Medium

This simple glaze can be used on any kind of poultry, especially duck. This would go well with squash or potatoes and asparagus or crisp tossed salad.

6 slices bacon, diced
2 tsp. minced fresh garlic
1/2 cup pure maple syrup
2 1/2 tsp. Worcestershire sauce

6 chicken breasts, boned and skinned
olive oil for brushing
coarse salt to taste
lots of black pepper, to taste

In a skillet, fry bacon on medium-high heat until crisp. Remove bacon bits with a slotted spoon and drain on paper towels. Drain 1/2 of the bacon grease into a cup and reserve. Lower heat to medium and cook garlic until just wilted but not brown. Remove skillet from heat and stir in maple syrup and Worcestershire sauce. At this point, taste and determine if you wish to add some of reserved bacon grease for richness; if not, discard extra grease. Place chicken breasts between waxed paper and pound with a meat mallet until about 1/2-inch thick. Brush breasts with olive oil and sprinkle with salt and lots of pepper. Fire up the grill and when coals are at medium, place breasts on grill. Cook for about 6 to 8 minutes per side, brushing on glaze when chicken is turned. Meat should be opaque in the center, with no pink color. Coat with glaze just before serving and serve remaining glaze alongside.

BARBECUED TURKEY

Servings: 12
Grill: Medium-hot

This is the common method for barbecuing whole turkey. Covering the grill gives the meat a smoky flavor and a dark brown skin. For the best flavor use hickory wood chips soaked according to directions on the package. For a variation, baste with your favorite bottled barbecue sauce instead of flavored butter.

1 turkey, 12 lb.
3 tbs. butter, melted
2 tbs. chopped fresh rosemary, thyme or sage, or 2 tsp. dried
salt and black pepper to taste
2 tbs. barbecue salt or seasoning salt
1/2 cup butter, melted
2 tbs. lemon juice
dash Worcestershire sauce

Remove packages from cavities of turkey. Rinse inside and out with cold running water and pat dry. Brush 3 tbs. melted butter over skin and sprinkle with rosemary or herb of choice, salt and pepper. Sprinkle main and neck cavities with barbecue salt. Truss bird with kitchen string to keep wings and legs tight to the body so they won't get charred and overcooked. Place a large drip pan under grill rack and surround with coals.

Fire up the grill and when coals are medium-hot, brush grill with oil and place turkey breast-side-up on grill over drip pan. Cover and cook for 1 hour.

In a small bowl, combine melted butter, lemon juice and Worcestershire sauce and use this sauce to baste turkey. Check turkey in 35 minutes and baste with sauce. Repeat after 35 minutes and start checking for doneness. An instant thermometer should register 170° in the breast meat or, when the thickest portion of the thigh is pierced, the liquid should run clear with no pink color. Total cooking time should be about $2\frac{1}{4}$ to $2\frac{1}{2}$ hours. Check coals and wood chips during the cooking process to make sure the temperature is being maintained. Allow bird to rest for 15 minutes before carving.

GARLIC CHICKEN

Servings: 6
Grill: Medium-hot

Garlic lovers really like this grilled chicken. Using thighs or breasts is a personal choice. Serve with creamy pasta and tossed salad or grilled potatoes, grilled vegetables and crisp coleslaw.

1/2 cup butter
4–5 tbs. finely minced onion
2 1/2 tsp. minced fresh garlic
1 cup beer
1 1/2 tbs. finely chopped parsley or
   cilantro

1/2 tsp. black pepper
dash salt, or to taste
6 whole legs chicken with thighs
   attached or whole breasts

In a saucepan, melt butter over medium heat. Add onion and garlic and sauté until onion is wilted and transparent, about 5 minutes. Stir in beer and bring to a boil. Remove from heat and stir in parsley, pepper and salt. Brush beer mixture on chicken pieces. Place a drip pan under grill rack and surround with coals. Fire up the grill and when coals are medium-hot, oil rack and place chicken skin-side up over drip pan. Cover and grill for about 40 minutes for legs or thighs or about 25 minutes for breasts. Turn and baste frequently until chicken is brown and center of meat is opaque with no pink color.

SEAFOOD

SEED-CRUSTED GRILLED TUNA

Servings: 6
Grill: Hot

Serve this as an appetizer, a main dish or mixed with greens in a salad. The seeds give this fish a wonderful toasted nut flavor and crunchy texture. Thinly slice and serve on bread or crackers as an appetizer along with a light wasabi cream or crushed olives. Serve as a main dish by slicing about 1/2-inch thick or serve in a green salad along with radishes, avocados, artichokes and/or olives.

3 tbs. sesame seeds
3 tbs. crushed coriander seeds
3 tbs. coarsely ground black pepper
2 lb. tuna loin
salt to taste
olive oil for brushing grill

In a small bowl, combine sesame seeds, coriander seeds and black pepper. Coat tuna with seed mixture, pressing gently. Sprinkle with salt. Fire up the grill and when coals are hot, brush grill with olive oil and cook for about 1 1/2 to 2 minutes on each side. The tuna should have a nice brown crust but be pink in the center. Remove from heat and chill. Serve as an appetizer, main dish or salad.

SEA SCALLOPS WITH LIME SAUCE

For this dish, sea scallops are wrapped in prosciutto, quickly grilled and served with a delicious creamy lime sauce. If prosciutto is not readily available, partially cooked bacon can be substituted.

1/2 cup chicken broth
1/2 cup dry white wine
2 tbs. lime juice
2 tbs. finely minced onions
1 1/2 tsp. grated fresh ginger
1 tsp. grated lime zest
1/2 cup cream

1/4 cup butter
1 1/2–2 lb. scallops, about 1 1/2 inch in
    diameter
1/4 lb. prosciutto, thinly sliced
bamboo skewers, soaked in water for
    1/2 hour
1/4 cup butter, melted

In a saucepan, combine broth, wine, lime juice, onions, ginger and lime zest. Bring to a boil uncovered and cook until mixture is reduced by half. Add cream and continue to cook until mixture thickens. Stir in butter until it melts; reserve. Rinse scallops and pat dry. Cut prosciutto to the width of scallop and wrap a piece around each scallop. Thread scallops onto 2 bamboo skewers. Fire up the grill and heat coals to medium. Baste scallops with melted butter. Place scallops on grill and turn every 3 minutes, basting each time, until brown and caramelized. The scallops should feel just firm to the touch: do not overcook. Serve with lime sauce.

SALMON WITH PIQUANT GREEN SAUCE

Servings: 6
Grill: Hot

For this dish, salmon is grilled to perfection and served with a pungent, piquant herb sauce. Make the sauce several hours in advance to allow flavors to mellow.

1 1/2 tbs. capers, drained
1 tsp. anchovy paste
3 stalks green onions, chopped
2 tbs. chopped fresh chives, or 2 tsp. dried
3 tbs. chopped fresh parsley or cilantro, or 1 tbs. dried
2 tbs. chopped fresh tarragon, or 2 tsp. dried
1 tsp. grated lemon zest
1 tbs. lemon juice
1/2 cup extra virgin olive oil
salt and pepper to taste
red wine vinegar to taste, optional
2 1/2 lb. salmon fillet, prefer King
olive oil for brushing
salt and pepper to taste

With a food processor or blender, blend together capers, anchovy paste, green onions, chives, parsley, tarragon, lemon zest and lemon juice. Slowly drizzle in olive oil until mix is emulsified. Taste and add salt and pepper to taste. Determine if you wish to add a little red wine vinegar to make mixture more tart. Allow to mellow for several hours before using.

Fire up the grill and when coals are hot, brush rack with oil. Brush salmon with olive oil and sprinkle with salt and pepper. Place salmon skin-side down on grill and cook for about 5 to 8 minutes, until meat has just turned opaque or you begin to see a white liquid ooze from meat. Remove from grill and serve with green sauce.

GRILLED SALMON AND ONION SANDWICH

Servings: 4
Grill: Medium

Grilled sourdough bread, grilled salmon and caramelized onions make an incredible sandwich. This would go well with chilled soup for summer or warm soup for winter along with a fruit dessert.

$^1/_2$ cup mayonnaise
3 tbs. minced fresh basil, or 1 tbs. dried
2 tsp. grated lemon zest
12 slices bacon
1 medium red onion, thinly sliced
$^1/_4$ cup olive oil
3 tbs. fresh basil, or 1 tbs. dried
$1^1/_2$ tbs. fresh lemon juice
pepper to taste
4 salmon fillets, 6 oz. each
8 slices sourdough bread
sliced tomatoes
lettuce leaves

In a small bowl, combine mayonnaise, basil, and lemon zest and set aside. In a large skillet, cook bacon on medium-high heat until crisp. Remove and drain on paper towels. Drain off all but 3 tbs. bacon grease and cook onion slices in same skillet until onions are tender and begin to caramelize. In a small bowl, combine olive oil, basil, lemon juice and pepper. Pour mixture over salmon, cover and refrigerate for at least 1 hour.

Fire up the grill and when coals are medium-hot, place fillets on the grill. Grill for about 3 minutes per side or until salmon begins to ooze white liquid. Brush one side of each slice of bread with olive oil mixture and grill until toasted on both sides. To assemble sandwich, spread mayonnaise on one side of each piece of bread. On 4 of the bread slices, evenly divide bacon, tomato slices, caramelized onions, salmon and lettuce. Top with remaining bread slices. You may want to keep this huge sandwich together with a long toothpick.

SPICY GRILLED PRAWNS

Servings: 4
Grill: Medium-hot

This is a quick and easy recipe where prawns are basted with a spicy compound butter. To prevent prawns from falling through the grill, either thread on skewers or use a grill basket. This dish would be good served with grilled polenta and either a crisp green salad or steamed green vegetables.

1/2 cup butter, melted
1 1/2 tbs. dry white wine or lemon juice
1 tbs. finely chopped fresh parsley or
  cilantro
1 tsp. finely minced fresh garlic
1/3 tsp. cayenne pepper

salt to taste
few dashes Tabasco Sauce
24 large prawns, shelled but with tail
  left on
bamboo skewers, soaked in water for
  30 minutes

In a bowl, mix together butter, wine, parsley, garlic, cayenne pepper, salt and Tabasco Sauce. Rinse prawns in cold water and pat dry. Thread 3 prawns on each skewer and baste with butter sauce. Leave prawns at room temperature for 30 minutes before grilling. Fire up the grill and when coals are medium-hot, place prawns on rack and grill, basting frequently, until prawns just turn pink and opaque, about 3 minutes per side. Remove from rack and serve 2 skewers per person.

GINGER SEA BASS

Servings: 4
Grill: Medium-hot

Sea bass is one of my favorite fish. It is important that you not overcook bass: the outside should be flaky but the inside should just barely be opaque. Serve with a flavorful rice side dish, steamed greens and a sinfully rich dessert.

1/2 cup butter
1 tbs. grated fresh ginger
2 tsp. finely minced fresh parsley
1 tsp. minced fresh garlic
1 1/2 tsp. lemon juice
1/8 tsp. white pepper
4 sea bass steaks

In a small saucepan, melt butter and add ginger, parsley, garlic, lemon juice and white pepper. Taste and adjust seasonings. Fire up the grill and when coals are medium-hot, brush a little of the butter mixture on steaks and place fish on rack. Cover grill and cook for about 7 to 8 minutes per side. Baste when turning. Baste one last time before serving.

SALMON BURGERS

Servings: 4
Grill: Medium-hot

This is a great, flavorful alternative to hamburgers. For variation use sprouts for lettuce, grilled red peppers for tomatoes and tartar sauce for mayonnaise.

1 tbs. butter
1 tbs. olive oil
1/2 cup chopped onion or shallot
1/2 cup dry white wine
1/4 cup capers, drained and chopped
1/4 cup fresh lemon juice
1 lb. skinless salmon fillets
1 1/2 cups fresh breadcrumbs
1 egg, beaten
2 tbs. fresh dill, or 2 tsp. dried
3/4 tsp. salt
1/4 tsp. black pepper
4 large hamburger buns, toasted
mayonnaise
lettuce
sliced tomatoes

In a skillet, heat butter and oil on medium-high heat, add onions and cook until onions are wilted. Add wine, capers and lemon juice and cook until most of the liquid has evaporated. Cool to room temperature and set aside. Remove any bones from salmon and chop coarsely. Mix chopped salmon with breadcrumbs, egg, dill, salt, pepper and caper mixture. Fry a small amount of mixture in a skillet. Taste and adjust seasonings. Form into patties, cover and refrigerate until ready to use.

Fire up the grill and when coals are medium-hot, brush grill with oil and place patties gently on the grill. If you have a grill skillet, use it to help keep burgers from crumbling. Cook until salmon turns pink throughout, about 2 to 3 minutes per side. Turn burgers only once and brush oil on rack when turning.

BLACKENED SWORDFISH

The rub for this recipe can be used on almost any fish. Swordfish is a very solid fish with texture that somewhat resembles steak. When grilling fish, it is important to have a well oiled grill rack. Blackened fish should have a dark-brown crust. Serve with a colorful rice pilaf and maybe steamed or grilled pea pods. For grilling pea pods, you need a grill basket.

1 tbs. paprika
1 tbs. minced fresh thyme, or 1 tsp. dried
1 1/2–2 tsp. salt, to taste
1 tsp. cayenne pepper

1 tsp. black pepper
1/2 tsp. finely minced fresh garlic
1/4 tsp. white pepper, or more to taste
4 swordfish fillets, 8 oz. each
melted butter for brushing

In a bowl, combine paprika, thyme, salt, cayenne pepper, black pepper, garlic and white pepper. Rinse fillets under cold water and pat dry. Liberally brush melted butter on fish and massage in rub on both sides. Fire up the grill and when coals are hot, brush a little oil on grill rack and cook fish for about 3 minutes on each side or until the center is just opaque.

ALDER-PLANKED SALMON

Servings: 4
Grill: Medium

Alder planks can be purchased at any major lumber yard. The wood should be rough-cut, 4 to 6 inches by 10 to 12 inches by about 1 inch thick. If desired, serve salmon with a pat of citrus butter or herb garlic butter. If this is your first time, season the board by rubbing it with olive oil and heating in a 350° oven for 30 minutes.

1/4 cup fresh lime juice
3 1/2 tbs. grated fresh ginger
3 tbs. soy sauce
1 1/2 tbs. toasted sesame oil
1 1/2 tsp. minced fresh garlic

1 1/2 tsp. turbinado or light brown sugar
several dashes Tabasco Sauce, or more
   to taste
1 pinch cayenne pepper, or to taste
1 1/2 lb. fresh salmon filet

In a bowl, combine lime juice, ginger, soy sauce, sesame oil, garlic, sugar, Tabasco Sauce and cayenne pepper. Cover salmon with lime mixture and marinate for 1 hour. Liberally coat the plank with olive oil. Place salmon skin-side down on plank. Pour any remaining marinade on top. Fire up the grill and when coals are at medium, place plank with fish on grill and cover. Salmon is done when a white, creamy liquid just begins to ooze out of fish: depending on thickness of salmon it should take about 35 minutes or more. Center of fish should be just opaque.

LOBSTER TAIL WITH WINE BUTTER SAUCE

Lobster is fantastic when barbecued: it takes on a slightly smoky taste that marries well with white wine butter sauce. Lobster cooks quickly, and it is very important not to overcook it. Meat should just turn opaque and be taken off the grill immediately.

1/3 cup minced shallots
1/3 cup dry white wine
1/4 cup fresh lemon juice
1 cup butter, softened
salt and white pepper to taste
1 pinch sugar
4 medium lobster tails

In a nonaluminum saucepan, combine shallots, white wine and lemon juice. Cook uncovered on medium-high heat for about 5 minutes or until most of the liquid has evaporated. Reduce heat to low and whisk in butter a little at a time until all butter has been incorporated. Add a small pinch of sugar, taste and adjust seasonings. Rinse each lobster tail and pat dry. Place on a cutting board shell-side down and cut in half lengthwise through shell. Place lobster pieces in a glass baking dish and spoon wine sauce on top. Marinate in wine butter sauce for 30 minutes before grilling.

Fire up the grill and when coals are medium-hot, oil grill rack, drain marinade from tails, place flesh-side down on grill and cook for 5 minutes. Turn tails flesh-side up and baste with marinade. Continue to cook for 3 to 5 minutes or until flesh just begins to turn opaque. Shell should turn bright red. Heat any remaining marinade and serve alongside immediately.

GRILLED VEGETABLES AND FRUITS

GRILLED ASPARAGUS AND MUSHROOMS

Servings: 4-6
Grill: Medium-hot

If you are unable to find pancetta, you can substitute prosciutto or unsmoked ham. You'll only need part of the flavored butter for this recipe. Cover and refrigerate remainder for up to 3 weeks. Use to flavor potatoes and vegetables or spread on bread.

12 large cloves of garlic
$\frac{1}{4}$ cup lean pancetta, finely chopped
$\frac{1}{4}$ cup butter
12–18 thick asparagus spears
extra virgin olive oil for brushing

sprinkling of coarse salt
$\frac{3}{4}$ lb. oyster or other mushrooms
1 tsp. lemon juice
$\frac{1}{4}$ cup chopped fresh parsley

In a small saucepan, cover garlic cloves with water and boil for 20 minutes. Drain, allow cloves to cool and peel. With a food processor or blender, puree garlic into a paste. Add pancetta and butter. Puree until completely mixed and set aside. Use a grill pan with holes to cook vegetables, or grill asparagus by threading about 6 spears at a 90° angle on two presoaked bamboo skewers. This will allow you to turn spears easily without them falling through grill. Brush asparagus with oil and sprinkle with coarse salt. Fire up the grill and when coals are medium-hot, cook until slightly charred and tender, about 8 to 10 minutes. Cut off any hard parts of mushroom, sprinkle with lemon and brush with oil. Grill until nicely brown and tender. Place hot grilled vegetables in a bowl and stir in about 1 to 2 tbs. garlic butter. Sprinkle with parsley and serve immediately.

GRILLED ZUCCHINI OR SUMMER SQUASH

Servings: 6
Grill: Medium-hot

This marinade can be used on all types of vegetables, especially bell peppers. The herbs can be changed to any combination you like. Don't leave the barbecue when grilling vegetables: they tend to cook quickly and can easily get over-charred.

$^1/_3$ cup olive oil
$^1/_8$ cup vinegar, prefer balsamic
1 $^1/_2$ tbs. chopped fresh cilantro, thyme or rosemary, or 1 $^1/_2$ tsp. dried
1 tbs. minced fresh garlic
salt and pepper to taste
4–6 small zucchini or summer squash

In a nonaluminum bowl, combine olive oil, vinegar, herbs, garlic, salt and pepper. Cut ends off zucchini and if there are large seeds, remove seeds with a spoon. Cut each zucchini in half lengthwise and cut each half into 2 to 3 long slivers; place in marinade.

Turn spears around in marinade so all sides are covered. Fire up the grill and when coals are medium-hot, place vegetables on rack. Turn vegetables frequently until tender-crisp, about 10 minutes.

136   GRILLED VEGETABLES AND FRUITS

GRILLED AVOCADO

Servings: 6
Grill: Medium-hot

Grilled avocados are a special and unusual treat. Serve one avocado half per person along with a spoon or cut up avocados, mash lightly and mix with a little chopped tomato. Serve on salad greens, as a chunky sauce with fajitas, or as a dip with chips.

1 1/2 tbs. fresh lemon juice
3 ripe Hass avocados
1 1/2 tbs. extra virgin olive oil
1 tbs. chopped fresh cilantro, parsley, basil or oregano
pepper to taste, optional

Leave skin on avocado, cut in half lengthwise and remove pit. Drizzle lemon juice on cut side of avocado and brush with olive oil. Fire up the grill and when coals are medium-hot, place avocado cut-side down about 6 inches from the grill. Grill for 2 minutes, turn over, add herbs and grill for an additional 2 to 3 minutes. Serve immediately.

CRISPY GRILLED POTATO SLICES

Servings: 4-6
Grill: Medium-hot

These potatoes are great with any grilled foods and cooks very quickly. Add a sprinkling of any of your favorite spices or herbs for endless variations. I usually leave the skin on for extra nutrition and flavor but that is optional.

4 large russet potatoes
olive oil for brushing
1 tbs. coarse sea salt or seasoning salt
2 tsp. minced fresh garlic
1 tsp. finely minced dried rosemary or herb of choice
pepper to taste

Wash potatoes, leave skin on and cut lengthwise into ¼-inch slices. Lay out slices on a baking sheet and brush with olive oil. Sprinkle salt, garlic, rosemary and pepper on slices, then turn them over and repeat. Fire up the grill and when coals are at low heat, lay slices on grill and close the cover. Cook for about 3 minutes per side, brushing with excess oil mixture left in baking sheet. Open grill, increase heat to medium-hot and grill until potatoes are crisp, turning frequently. Potatoes are done when fork-tender.

SMOKY CORN SOUP

Servings: 6
Grill: Medium-hot

Corn is cooked on the grill to give it that special barbecue flavor. This soup is loaded with bacon and potatoes and should be served with dense hot bread.

6 ears corn
2 quarts chicken stock
2 bay leaves
1/2 lb. bacon, diced
2 medium onions, diced

2 cups diced potatoes
1/4 cup chopped fresh thyme, or
   3–4 tsp. dried
salt and pepper to taste
1 tbs. chopped parsley

Husk and desilk corn. Heat a pot of water to boiling, add corn and cook for 2 minutes. Plunge corn in cold water to stop the cooking process. Pat corn dry with a paper towel. Fire up the grill and when coals are medium-hot, brush oil on rack and cook corn until golden brown on all sides, about 4 to 5 minutes. Remove from heat, cut kernels off cob and set aside. Place cobs in a large saucepan and add chicken stock and bay leaves. Bring to a boil, reduce heat, simmer and cook, covered, for 1 hour. Meanwhile, fry bacon in skillet on medium-high heat until brown. Drain on paper towels. Leave 3 to 4 tbs. grease in skillet. Fry onions on medium heat until wilted, about 5 minutes. Add corn kernels and cook for 4 minutes. Remove cobs from chicken stock and add onion-corn mixture, potatoes, thyme, salt and pepper. Cook over medium heat until potatoes are fork-tender, about 35 to 40 minutes. Just before serving, stir in parsley and cooked bacon. Taste and adjust seasoning.

SWEET ONION SLICES

Servings: 4-6
Grill: Medium

If you have access to Walla Walla sweet onions or Vidalia onions use these because they already have a wonderful sweet flavor. Otherwise I like to use red onions.

1/2 cup extra virgin olive oil
2 1/4 tbs. white wine, cider, or champagne vinegar
1 tbs. honey mustard or other sweet mustard
1 1/2 tbs. honey
1/4 tsp. salt
1 pinch white pepper
2 large red onions

Combine oil, vinegar, mustard, honey, salt and white pepper in a glass baking dish. Peel onions and cut into thick slices (about 1/2-inch). Place onions in marinade and gently spoon marinade over all. Marinate for 45 minutes at room temperature. Fire up the grill and when coals are at medium, place drained onion slices on grill. Cook for about 5 minutes on each side, until brown and tender.

ORANGE-FLAVORED FENNEL

Servings: 4-6
Grill: Medium-low

Fennel is a bulb that looks something like celery but has the subtle taste of anise. The marinade can be used for grilling almost any vegetable or poultry. This is a great vegetable to accompany pork, beef or poultry dishes.

1 cup orange juice
2 tbs. extra virgin olive oil
1 tbs. orange marmalade
$\frac{1}{2}$ tsp. salt
pepper to taste, optional
3 medium fennel bulbs

With a food processor or blender, puree orange juice, oil, marmalade, salt and pepper together until smooth. Cut the tops off fennel bulbs then cut each bulb lengthwise into 4 slices (cutting through stem). Pour marinade on fennel slices and marinate at room temperature for at least 30 minutes. Fire up the grill and when coals are medium-low, drain slices and place on grill. Cover and cook for about 10 minutes, turning only a few times but basting with marinade each time. The fennel should be soft to the touch when done.

MARINATED GRILLED LEEKS

Servings: 4
Grill: Medium-hot

This makes a great side dish for beef, poultry and seafood. An alternative to this recipe is to wrap leeks in prosciutto after marinating but before grilling.

$^1/_4$ cup extra virgin olive oil
$^1/_3$ cup white wine vinegar or
   champagne vinegar
1 tbs. grated orange zest
$^1/_3$ tsp. dried thyme

white pepper to taste
2–3 large leeks
bamboo skewers, soaked in water for
   20 minutes
$^1/_2$ cup shredded Parmesan cheese

In a bowl, combine oil, vinegar, orange zest, thyme and white pepper. Trim tough upper leaves from leeks leaving about 3 inches of green. Trim roots and split leeks in half lengthwise. Wash out grit from between layers. Thread a skewer through leaves to help keep leeks together during grilling. Place in a glass baking dish and pour marinade on top. Marinate leeks for at least 30 minutes. Fire up the grill and when coals are medium-hot, place drained leeks on grill and cook until brown and tender, about 12 minutes. Remove from grill and immediately sprinkle with Parmesan cheese.

GRILLED SEASONED GRAPES

Servings: 6
Grill: Medium-hot

This unusual treat will wow your guests! If you have whole rosemary stems, either twist the stems into the grape clusters or cook alongside the clusters. The smell of cooking rosemary is divine.

2 lb. seedless grapes, left on branches
1/4 cup extra virgin olive oil
1/8 tsp. crushed rosemary
1/8 tsp. crushed sage

Wash grapes and allow to air-dry. In a small bowl, mix together olive oil, rosemary and sage. Brush branches of grapes with olive oil mixture. Fire up the grill and when coals are at medium to medium-hot, place grapes about 6 inches from the coals. Turn grapes frequently and grill for about 20 minutes or until grapes just begin to split. Serve immediately.

NUTTY CARAMEL APPLES

Servings: 6
Grill: Medium

If you wish to save time, use purchased caramel sauce in place of the first 5 ingredients. The alcohol is optional: 1 tsp. vanilla can be substituted. Serve grilled apples alone or over vanilla ice cream.

$1/2$ cup butter
2 cups brown sugar, packed
$1/4$ cup apple brandy, bourbon or Frangelico liqueur, optional
$1/3$ tsp. cinnamon
$2/3$ cup whipping cream
6 large apples, prefer Newton or Pippin
melted butter
skewers
$3/4$ cup chopped toasted pecans

In a heavy saucepan, melt butter, add sugar, brandy and cinnamon and stir to combine. Bring mixture to a boil over medium heat and boil for 2 minutes, stirring frequently. Remove saucepan from heat and gently stir in cream. If mixture thickens too much for spooning, add a little water or more cream. Peel, core and cut apples into thick wedges. Use either metal skewers, presoaked bamboo skewers or a metal grill basket to cook apples. Thread wedges onto skewers and baste with melted butter.

Fire up the grill and when coals are at medium, cook apples uncovered for about 10 minutes total, occasionally turning and basting with more butter. Just before serving, baste apples with caramel sauce and cook for 1 minute on each side, basting when you turn. Push apples off skewers and sprinkle with nuts.

SWEET GRILLED BANANAS

Servings: 6
Grill: Medium

Serve grilled bananas on ice cream or as a side dish with pork, poultry or fish. If you are going to use this as a caramelized banana split, I would include chopped peanuts, pecans or almonds for crunch.

1 cup sugar
2/3 cup cream
6 tbs. butter
few drops banana or vanilla extract
6 medium bananas

In a saucepan, combine sugar and cream and bring to a boil. Stir in butter, reduce heat to medium and cook for a few minutes until mixture thickens slightly. Remove pan from heat and stir in banana extract. Slice bananas in half lengthwise. Fire up the grill and when coals are at medium, oil grill rack and place bananas on the grill cut-side down. Cook for 3 to 4 minutes. Turn bananas skin-side down and brush with cream mixture. Grill for about 3 minutes and serve with a little of the cream sauce on top.

GRILLED LIME PINEAPPLE

This recipe can be used as a side dish or a dessert. The natural sugar in fruit comes out and caramelizes on the surface. Pineapple is sturdy and keeps its shape and texture when grilling. For a variation, cut up the pineapple after grilling and spoon it over vanilla ice cream with a little of the sauce.

$1/3$ cup fresh lime juice
$1/3$ cup light corn syrup
$1 1/4$ tsp. dried mint
1 tsp. brown sugar
$1/2$ tsp. fresh ground black pepper
2 pineapples
3 tbs. chopped fresh mint leaves

In a small saucepan, mix together lime juice, corn syrup, dried mint, brown sugar and pepper. Cook over medium heat for 5 to 6 minutes, stirring occasionally. Remove from heat and set aside while grilling pineapple. Peel pineapple and cut into 1-inch rounds: you should be able to get about 8 rounds per pineapple. Fire up the grill and when coals are at medium, brush oil on rack and grill pineapple slices about 4 to 5 minutes per side. Just before serving, brush on lime mixture and serve. Add fresh mint leaves to remaining sauce and serve alongside.

INDEX

Beef, continued
　steak with green salsa 102
　teriyaki marinade 28
　wine-marinated tenderloin 84
Beer chicken 108
Blackened beef salad 72
Blackened swordfish 130
Brazier 2
Bruschetta, portobello
　　mushroom 22
Burger(s)
　island 98
　Mexi- 88
　Parmesan basil 95
　salmon 128
Butter
　citrus 43
　garlic mustard 45
　Gorgonzola 48
　Greek 46
　herb garlic 42
　lemon mint 44
　tarragon 47

C
Cajun chicken salad 66
Charcoal grill technique 5
Charcoal, hardwood 6
Cheese
　grilled in grape leaves 17
　quesadillas 13
　and tomato pizza, grilled 20
Chicken
　beer 108
　breast, tandoori 110
　Buffalo wings 12
　fajitas 106
　garlic 118
　ginger plum drumettes 15
　lemon 109
　lime soup 18
　mango salad 76
　maple 115
　with mint chutney 105
　salad, Cajun 66
　sesame 112
　wings, ginger 114
Chutney, mango 58

Chutney, mint, with chicken
　105
Cilantro lamb rub 38
Citrus butter 43
Clams and mussels, grilled 16
Cleaning grill 8
Cola barbecue sauce 57
Corn soup, smoky 139
Curried cilantro mayonnaise 59

D
Dill seafood rub 35

E
Electric countertop grill 2
Electric smoker 3

F
Fajita, beef 82
Fajitas, chicken 106
Fennel, orange-flavored 141
Fire starters 6

W

Water smoker 4

Wild game marinade, orange
30

Wine
  and apricot marinade 32
  -marinated beef tenderloin
    84
  poultry marinade 29

Wood chips 6

Y

Yogurt marinade, Indian 31

Z

Zucchini or summer squash,
  grilled 136

Serve Creative, Easy, Nutritious Meals with nitty gritty® Cookbooks

100 Dynamite Desserts
The 9 x 13 Pan Cookbook
The Barbecue Cookbook *(new)*
Beer and Good Food
The Best Bagels are Made at Home
The Best Pizza is Made at Home*(new)*
Bread Baking
Bread Machine Cookbook
Bread Machine Cookbook II
Bread Machine Cookbook III
Bread Machine Cookbook IV
Bread Machine Cookbook V
Bread Machine Cookbook VI
Cappuccino/Espresso
Casseroles *(new)*
The Coffee Book
Convection Oven Cookery *(new)*
Cooking for 1 or 2
Cooking in Clay
Cooking in Porcelain
Cooking with Chile Peppers
Cooking with Grains
Cooking with Your Kids
Creative Mexican Cooking
Deep Fried Indulgences

The Dehydrator Cookbook
Easy Vegetarian Cooking
Edible Pockets for Every Meal
Entrées From Your Bread Machine
Extra-Special Crockery Pot Recipes
Fabulous Fiber Cookery
Fondue and Hot Dips
Fresh Vegetables
From Freezer, 'Fridge and Pantry
From Your Ice Cream Maker
The Garlic Cookbook
Gourmet Gifts
Healthy Cooking on the Run
Healthy Snacks for Kids
Indoor Grilling
The Juicer Book
The Juicer Book II
Lowfat American Favorites
Marinades
Muffins, Nut Breads and More
The New Blender Book
New International Fondue Cookbook
No Salt, No Sugar, No Fat
One-Dish Meals
Oven and Rotisserie Roasting

Party Fare
The Pasta Machine Cookbook
Pinch of Time: Meals in Less than 30 Minutes
Quick and Easy Pasta Recipes
Recipes for the Loaf Pan
Recipes for the Pressure Cooker
Recipes for Yogurt Cheese
Risottos, Paellas, and other Rice Specialties
The Sandwich Maker Cookbook
The Sensational Skillet: Sautés and Stir-Fries *(new)*
Slow Cooking in Crock-Pot,® Slow Cooker, Oven and Multi-Cooker
The Steamer Cookbook
The Toaster Oven Cookbook
Unbeatable Chicken Recipes
The Versatile Rice Cooker
Waffles
The Well Dressed Potato
The Wok
Worldwide Sourdoughs from Your Bread Machine
Wraps and Roll-Ups

For a free catalog, call: Bristol Publishing Enterprises, Inc.
(800) 346-4889
www.bristolcookbooks.com